Nobel Laureates
in Literature
1901-2014

Sam Majdi

ISBN-10: 1511476591
ISBN-13: 978-1511476591

ACKNOWLEDGMENTS

I am grateful to my wife and children who have been really supportive and caring when I needed them most. I am also thankful to Mr. Gordon A. Kessler who has helped, guided me and made publishing this book possible. The author has made use of different sources to write this book. The most important of them are the following:

The Universal Standard Encyclopedia. An Abridgment of the New Funk and Wagnalls Encyclopedia prepared under the editorial direction of Joseph Laffan Morse, Sc.B., LL.B., LL.D. Editor in Chief. Standard Reference Works Publishing Company , Inc., New York © 1956 and 1957 By Wilfred Funk, Inc. Copyright Under the Articles of Copyright Convention of the Pan-American, Republics and the United States. IEF. 25 volumes Printed in the United States of America All Rights Reserved.

Academic American Encyclopedia Library of Congress Cataloging-in-Publication Data Includes bibliographical references and index ISBN 0-7172-5060-5 Copyright © 1996 by Grolier Inc. 21 volumes printed and manufactured in the United States of America. All rights reserved. No part of this book may be reproduced or transmitted in any form by any means electronic, mechanical, or otherwise, whether now or hereafter devised, including photocopying, recording, or by any information storage and retrieval system without express written prior permission from the publisher.

Colliers Encyclopedia with Bibliography and Index William D. Halsey Editorial Director Lois Shores, Ph.D. Editor In Chief Robert H. Blackburn, M.A., B.L.S., M.S. LL.D. Consultant for Canada. Sir Frank Francis,, K.C.B., M.A., D.LITT. F.S.A. Consultant For Great Britain. Copyright © Macmillan Educational

The author has also made use of Wikipedia and Britannica.com

Introduction

Any of the Nobel Prizes (5 in number until 1969, when the 6th was added that are awarded annually by four institutions (3 Swedish and one Norwegian) from a fund established under the will of Alfred Bernhard Nobel.

Distribution began on December 10, 1901, the fifth anniversary of the death of the founder, whose will specified that the rewards should be made "to those who, during the preceding year, shall have conferred the greatest benefit on mankind."

The five prizes are the Nobel Prize for physics; the Nobel Prize for chemistry; the Nobel Prize for physiology or medicine; the Nobel Prize for literature; and the Nobel Prize for peace.

An additional award, the Prize for Economic Sciences in Memory of Alfred Nobel, was set up in 1968 by the Bank of Sweden, and the first award was given in 1969.

The institutions cited as a prize awarders are the Royal Swedish Academy of Sciences (physics and chemistry), the Royal Caroline Institute (physiology or medicine), and the Swedish Academy (literature)—all in Stockholm—and the Norwegian Nobel Committee (peace), located in Oslo.

A prize is either given to one person or shared jointly by two or three persons. The prize can be awarded more than once to the same recipient.

Between 1901 and 2014, the Nobel Prizes and the Prize in Economic Sciences were awarded 561 times to 889 people and organizations. A person or organization awarded the Nobel Prize is called Nobel Laureate. The word "Laureate" refers to being signified by the laurel wreath. In ancient Greece, laurel wreaths were awarded to victors as a sign of honor. As of 2012, each prize was worth 1.2 million dollars. The cash prize is accompanied by a diploma and a gold medal. All the gold Nobel Prize medallions bear the profile of Alfred Nobel on the front. All except the economics medal, have a symbolic representation of the recipient's field of work on the back.

The exact weight of medal varies, but each medal is 18 karat green gold plated with 24 karat (pure) gold, with an average weight of 175 grams.

The Nobel Foundation was founded as a private organization on June 29, 1900.

The Nobel Prize and Prize in Economic Sciences have been awarded to women 47 times between 1901 and 2014. Only one woman, Marie Curie, has been awarded twice, the 1903 Nobel Prize in physics and the 1915 Nobel Prize in chemistry.

The awards in medicine and physiology, literature, physics and chemistry bear the same profile of Nobel. The profile on the peace and economics medals are slightly different.

The Nobel Prize in literature was not awarded in 1914, 1918, 1935, 1940, 1941, 1942, and 1943 because of World War I and World War II.

The medal of Swedish Academy (literature) represents a young man sitting under a laurel tree who, enchanted, listens to and writes the song of the Muse.

The inscription reads: Inventas vitam juvat excoluisse per artes "And they who bettered life on earth by their newly found mastery."

The Nobel Prize has been awarded to 111 Nobel Laureates in Literature since 1901.

107 Nobel Prizes in Literature have been awarded since (1901-2014). 13 women have been awarded so far. Four literature Prizes have been divided between two persons.

42 years was the age of the youngest Literature Laureate ever, Rudyard Kipling, best known for Jungle Book. 88 years was the age of the oldest Literature Laureate ever, Doris Lessing, when she was awarded the Prize in 2007. 64 is the average age of the Nobel Laureates in Literature the year they were awarded the prize.

Names Index

Seamus **Heaney**	1995	93	1939-2013
Carl Gustaf Verner Von			
Heidenstam	1916	17	1859-1940
Earnest Miller **Hemingway**	1954	50	1899-1961
Hermann **Hesse**	1946	42	1877-1962
Paul Johann Ludwig			
Von **Heyse**	1910	12	1830-1914
Elfriede **Jelinek**	2004	102	1946...
Johannes Vilhelm **Jensen**	1944	40	1873-1950
Juan Ramón **Jiménez**			
Mantecón	1956	52	1881-1958
Eyvind **Johnson**	1974	72	1900-1976
Erik Axel **Karlfeldt**	1931	32	1864-1931
Yasunari **Kawabata**	1968	65	1899-1972
Irme **Kertész**	2002	100	1929...
Joseph Rudyard **Kipling**	1907	9	1865-1936
Pär Fabian **Lagerkvist**	1951	47	1891-1974
Selma Ottilia Lovisa			
Lagerlöf	1909	11	1858-1940
Halldór Kiljan Lexness	1955	51	1902-1998
Jean-Marie Gustave **Le**			
Clézio	2008	106	1940...
Doris May **Lessing**	2007	105	1919-2013
Harry Sinclair **Lewis**	1930	31	1885-1951
Octavio Paz **Lozano**	1990	88	1914-1998
Salvatore **Quasimodo**	1959	55	1901-1968
Maurice Polydore Marie Bernard			
Maeterlinck (Comte Count)	1911	13	1682-1949
Naguib **Mahfouz**	1988	86	1911-2006
Thomas **Mann**	1929	30	1875-1955
Gabriel José de la Concordia			
García **Márquez**	1982	80	1927-2014
Martin du Gard	1937	37	1881-1958
Harry Edmund **Martinson**	1974	71	1904-1978
François Charles **Mauriac**	1952	48	1885-1970
Czeslaw **Milosz**	1980	78	1911-2004
Frédéric **Misteral**	1904	6	1830-1914
Gabriela Lucila Godoy			
Alcayaga **Mistral**	1945	41	1889-1957
Jean Patrick **Modiano**	2014	112	1945...
Christian Matthias Theodor			
Mommsen	1902	3	1817-1903
Eugenio **Montale**	1975	73	1896-1981
Toni **Morrison** (chloe Ardelia			
Wofford)	1975	73	1896-1981
Herta **Müller**	2009	107	1953...

Alice Ann **Munro**	2013	111	1931...
Sir Vidiadhar Surajprasad "V.S." **Naipal**	2001	99	1932...
Pablo **Neruda** (Neftali Ricardo Reyes Basoalto)	1971	68	1904-1973
Kenzaburō **Ōe**	1994	92	1935...
Eugene Gladstone **O'Neill**	1936	36	1888-1953
Ferit Orhan **Pamuk**	2000	104	1952...
Boris Leonidovich **Pasternak**	1958	54	1890-1960
Octavio **Paz** Lozano	1990	88	1914-1998
Saint-John **Perse** (Alexis Leger)	1960	56	1887-1975
Harold **Pinter**	2005	103	1930-2008
Luigi **Pirandello**	1934	35	1867-1936
Henik **Pontoppidian**	1917	19	1857-1943
René François Armand (Sully **Prudhomme**)	1901	2	1839-1907
Salvatore **Quasimodo**	1959	55	1901-1968
Wladyslaw Stanislaw **Reymont**	1924	25	1867-1925
Romain **Rolland**	1915	16	1866-1944
Bertrand Arthur William **Russell** 3rd Earl Russell	1950	46	1872-1970
Nelly Leonie **Sachs**	1966	62	1891-1970
José de Sousa **Samarago**	1998	96	1922-2010
Jean-Paul Charles Aymard **Sartre**	1964	60	1905-1980
Giorgos (George) **Seferis**	1963	59	1900-1971
Jaroslav **Seifert**	1984	82	1901-1981
George Bernard **Shaw**	1925	26	1856-1950
Mikhail Aleksanrovich **Sholokhov**	1965	61	1905-1984
Henrik Adam Alexander Pius **Sienkiewicz**	1905	7	1846-1916
Frans Eemil **Sillanpää**	1939	39	1888-1964
Claude **Simon**	1985	83	1913-2005
Isaac Bashevis Singer	1978	76	1902-1991
Wole **Soyinka** (Akinwande Oluwole)	1986	84	1934...
Carl Friedrich Georg **Spitteler**	1919	20	1845-1924
Aleksandr Isayevich **Solzhenitsyn**	1970	67	1818-2008
John Ernst **Steinbeck**, Jr.	1962	58	1902-1968
Wislawa **Szymboroska**	1996	94	1923-2012

Sir Rabindranath **Tagore** (Takhur)	1913	15	1861-1941
Thomas Gösta **Tranströmer**	2011	109	1931...
Sigrid **Undset**	1928	29	1882-1949
Jorge Mario Pedro **Vargas** Llosa First Marquis of Vargas Llosa	2010	108	1936...
Derek Alton **Walcott**	1992	90	1930...
Patrick Victor Martindale **White**	1973	70	1912-1990
Gao **Xingjian**	2000	98	1940...
Guan Moye (Mo **Yan**)	2012	110	1955...
William Butler **Yeats**	1923	24	1865-1939

Alfred Bernhard Nobel

(October 21, 1833-December 10, 1896)

B. Stockholm, Sweden

D. Sanremo, Italy

Swedish chemist, engineer, innovator, armaments manufacturer, whose most important invention, the explosive dynamite, earned a fortune for him and provided the financial basis for the establishment of the Nobel Prize. His father Immanuel Nobel was an engineer and inventor who built bridges and buildings in Stockholm. He was educated in St. Petersburg, Russia. He traveled as a youth and returned to St. Petersburg in 1852 to assist his father. With his father he began to manufacture Nitroglycerin in a factory near Stockholm in 1862. An explosion in 1864 killed five people, among them Nobel's young brother, Emil. As a young man, Nobel studied with chemist Nikolai Zinin; then in 1850, went to Paris to further the work. At 18, he went to the United States for four years to study chemistry. Nobel left most of his fortune to a foundation established for the awarding of the prizes that bear his name. The prizes, awarded since 1901, are administered by the Nobel Foundation in Stockholm, Sweden. The prizes designated in Nobel's will were for physics, chemistry, physiology or medicine, literature, and peace. In 1969 a prize for economics endowed by the Central Bank of Sweden was added. Recipients in physics, Chemistry, and economics are named by the Royal Swedish Academy of Sciences; those in physiology or medicine by the Caroline Institute; those in literature by the Swedish Academy; and those who contribute to peace by Norwegian Nobel Committee appointed by Norwegian Parliament. The average value of each prize began at about $ 30,000 and was about $1million in 1995. Nobel laureates in literature have included historians, critics, and philosophers as well as novelists, dramatists, and essayists.

1901

René François Armand (Sully Prudhomme)

(March 16, 1839-September 6, 1907)

B. Paris, France

D. Châtenay, France

French poet and essayist. In writing poetry, he declared it as his interest to create scientific poetry for modern times. The Nobel Prize was awarded: "in special recognition of his poetic composition, which gives evidence of lofty idealism, artistic perfection and a rare combination of the qualities of both heart and intellect"

He wanted to become an engineer, but an eye disease terminated his training at a polytechnic institute. He studied literature, and after a brief and unsuccessful interlude in industry, he took up law. He was a member of the 'Conference La Bruyère', a distinguished student society, and the favorable reception that his fellow members gave to his juvenilia encouraged him to go on writing poetry. His fist volume, Stances et Poèmes (Stanzas and Poems, 1865), was well reviewed by Sainte-Beuve and established his reputation. He combined perfection and elegance with philosophic and scientific interests. A collected edition of his writings in five volumes appeared in 1900-01. He also wrote essays and a book on Pascal, La Vraie Religion selon Pascal (Pascal on True Religion, 1905). He was a member of the French Academy from 1881 until his death in 1907.

He devoted the bulk of money he received to the creation of a poetry prize awarded by Société des gens de lettres. He also founded the Société des poetès français with Jose-Maria de Herodia and Leon Dierx.

His works: Corquis Italiens (Italian Notebooks, 1866-68); Solitudes (1869); Impressions de la querre (Impressions of Flowers, 1870); Les Destins (Destinies, 1872); La Révolte des fleurs (Revolt of the Flowers, 1872); and Les Vaines Tenderness (Vain Endearments, 1875)

1902

Christian Matthias Theodor Mommsen

(Nov. 30, 1817-Nov. 1, 1903)

B. Garding, Schelwig, Germany

D. Charlottenburg, Germany

German classical scholar, historian, journalist, archeologist and writer generally regarded as the greatest classicist of the 19th century.

"The greatest living master of the art of historical writing, with special reference to his monumental work, A History of Rome"

He was also a prominent German politician, as a member of the Russian and German parliaments. He studied Greek and Latin and received his diploma in 1837, with the degree of Doctor of Roman Law. As he could not afford to study at one of the more prestigious German Universities, he enrolled at the University of Kiel in Holstein. He studied jurisprudence at Kiel from 1838 to 1843. In 1852 he obtained a professorship in Roman law at the University of Zurich. In 1834 he became a professor of law at the University of Breslau. He also became a research professor at the Berlin Academy of Sciences in 1857. He published over 1500 works, and effectively established a new framework for the systematic study of Roman history.

He later helped to create and manage the German Archeological Institute in Rome. His work regarding Roman history (1854-85) is still of fundamental importance for contemporary research. He was also involved in German politics, serving in Reichstag from 1881 to 1884, and his work often reflects his own desire for Germany.

His books include Römisches Staatsrecht (Roman Constitutional Law, 1871-88 and Römisches Strafrecht (Roman Criminal Law, 1899); The Provinces of the Roman Empire,1885); and Roman Chronology to the Time of Caesar (1858); written with his brother August; and Roman Constitutional Law (1871-88).

1903

Bjørnstjerne Martinus Bjørnson

(December 8, 1832-April 26, 1910)

B. Kvikne, Norway

D. Paris, France

Norwegian poet, novelist, playwright, and lyricist.

He is considered one of The Great Four Norwegian writers, the others being Henrik Ibsen, Jonas Lie, and Alexander Kielland.

"as a tribute to his noble, magnificent and versatile poetry, which has always been distinguished by both the freshness of its inspiration, and the rare purity of its spirit"

He was sent to Heltbergs Studentfabrikk in Christania to prepare for university, at the age of 17. He had realized that he wanted to pursue his talent for poetry (he had written verses since age 7). He matriculated at the University of Oslo in 1852, soon embarking upon a career as a journalist, focusing on criticism of drama. Early in 1865 he undertook the management of Christiania theatre, and brought out his popular comedy De Nygifte (The Newly Married) and his romantic tragedy of Mary Stuart in Scotland. He is celebrated for his lyrics to the Norwegian National Anthem. In his writing, he extols the virtues of Norwegian culture and examines international social issues. His poem 'Ja vi elsker dette landet' (Yes, We Love This Country), is used as Norway's National Anthem. He achieved an international reputation with dramas concerning social and political problems, notably the Editor (1874) and The Bankrupt (1875). His commitments to the ideals of humanism made him tireless and increasingly influential spokesman for the rights of individuals and minorities throughout Europe.

Some other works: Poetic trilogy Sigurd Slembe (Sigurd the Bad), 1862); Magnhild (1877); and Kaptejn Mansana (Captain Mansana, 1878).

1904

José Echegaray y Eizaguirre

(April 19, 1832-September 14, 1916)

B. Madrid, Spain

D. Madrid, Spain

Spanish civil engineer, mathematician, statesman, and the leading Spanish dramatist of the last quarter of the 19th century.

"in recognition of the numerous and brilliant compositions which, in an individual and original manner, have revived the great traditions of the Spanish drama"

He went to an engineering school, studied economy, and had a distinguished career in the Spanish Government. At the height of his career he turned to the stage, a passion that dated back to his youth. A professor of mathematics in early life, he entered government service in 1868, holding various positions. He was named Minister of Finance in 1874 and played a major role in developing the Banco de España. His early work is almost wholly Romantic, but, under the influence of Henrik Ibsen and others, he turned to thesis drama in his later work. He was a romantic writer with a tendency toward melodramatic, highly emotional themes. He shared the Nobel Prize for literature with Frédéric Mistral. His most famous play is El gran Galeoto, a drama written in the grand 19th century manner of melodrama. It is about the poisonous effect that unfounded gossip has on a middle-man's happiness. Paramount Pictures filmed it as a silent with the title changed to The World and His Wife. Although his plays seem somewhat affected today, they are still appreciated for their vigor, psychological depth, and mastery of dramatic technique. The Echegaray Street named after him in Madrid is famed for its famous Flamenco taverns. His most remarkable plays are Saint or Madman? (O Locura o santidad, 1877); Mariana (1892); El estigma (1895); and El Loco Dios (A Madman Divine, 1900).

1904

Frédéric Mistral

(September 8, 1830-March 25, 1914)

B. Maillane, France

D. Maillane, France

His genius for depicting rural life, his lyric and imaginative gifts, and his passionate love gave him an international stature. He had a brilliant scholastic career, taking honors at the law school in Aix. He was not only the greatest poet in the Langue d'oc (Provençal), but also helped restore and purify that ancient language.

"in recognition of the fresh originality and true inspiration of his poetic production, which faithfully reflects the natural scenery and native spirit of his people, and, in addition, his significant work as a Provençal philologist"

He studied law and in 1854 helped found the Félibrige, an association devoted to promoting the language and literature of Provence. His verse romance Mirèio (1859), was immediately recognized as a masterpiece and later adapted by the composer Charles Gounod as an opera; Mireille (1884), based on a medieval legend, was almost equally popular. His other works include an epic, Lou Pouèmo dóu Rose (1897), and collections of short poems. He is the author of Lou Tresor dóu Félibrige (The Treasury of the Félbrige, a Provençal dictionary, 1878-86), which to date remains the richest dictionary of the language Occitan, and one of most reliable for the precision of the directions. It is bilingual dictionary Occitan-French, in two great volumes. He also set up a museum in Arles Illustrating Provençal Life (1904).

Other works: His epic poem, Calendau (1867); Lis Isclo d'or (The Golden Isles); and his last great work was to collect, arrange and house at Arles (with the Nobel Prize money) the Museum Arlaten—a superb record of the lives, dwellings, crafts, art, religion, and festivals of the people of Provence.

1905

Henryk Adam Alexander Pius

Sienkiewicz, also known as Litwos

(May 5, 1846-Nov 15, 1916)

B. Wola Okrzejska, Congress, Poland

D. Vevey, Switzerland

Polish journalist, one of the most popular Polish writers at the turn of the 19th and 20th centuries.

"because of his outstanding merits as an epic writer"

He graduated from the University of Warsaw in 1870 and then began a career in journalism. From 1876 to 1878 he lived in the U.S., studying the problems of Polish immigrants. His travel to America provided him material for several works, among them the brilliant short story Latarnik (Lighthouse Keeper, 1882). His early works are satirized sketches, betraying a strong social conscience. According to his parent's wishes, he passed the examination to the medical department of Warsaw University. His works were noted for their negative portrayal of the portion of his readership lived under German rule. He was immensely popular. In 1900, a national subscription raised enough funds to buy him the castle in which his ancestors had lived. He is perhaps best known internationally for Quo Vadis (1896), a novel about persecution of the Christians under Nero in Rome. It has been dramatized and filmed a number of times. Poland's 17th century struggle of existence was pictured in his trilogy With Fire Sword (1884), The Deluge (1886), and Fire in the Steppe (1888).

Other works: Na Mame (in Vain, 1871); Hania (1876); The Teutonic Knights (The Knights of the Cross, 1900); In Desert and Wilderness (1912); Without Dogma (1891); Rodzina Polanieckich (1894); Krzyzacy (1900); Na polu chwaly (On the Field of Glory, 1906); and Wiry (Whirlpools, 1910). The complete edition of his works published 1948-55 runs to 60 volumes.

1906

Giosuè Alessandra Giuseppe Carducci

(July 27, 1835-February 16, 1907)

B. Val di castello, Tuscany, Italy

D. Bologna, Italy

Italian poet, scholar, and critic, often reckoned one of Italy's greatest. He was very influential and was regarded as the unofficial natural poet of modern Italy.

"not only in consideration of his deep learning and critical research, but above all as a tribute to the creative energy, freshness of style, and lyrical force which characterize his poetic masterpieces"

The son of a republican country doctor, he spent his childhood in the wild Maremma region of Southern Tuscany. He was early attracted to the Greek and Roman authors. Inspired both by his own time as well as by his study of the classical and Italian poets, he began writing poetry when he was a child. The first two collections of his poetry were Rime (Rhymes, 1857), and Levia Gravia (Light and Heavy, 1868). At the age of 20 he graduated with a degree in philosophy and letters from the University of Pisa. After several years in which he taught in various high schools, he was appointed to the chair of Italian Literature at the University of Bologna, a post that he held until his retirement in 1904. From the time he was in college, he was fascinated with the restrained style of Greek and Roman antiquity. He was also an excellent translator, and the lyrics of Goethe and Heine greatly influenced the development of his own poetry. He was an atheist and wrote " I know neither truth of God nor peace with the Vatican or any priests. They are the real and unfaltering enemies of Italy." In addition to his fame as a poet he was a noted literary historian and an eminent orator. He was a popular lecturer and a fierce critic of literature. While Inno a Satana had quite a revolutionary impact, Carducci's finest poetry came in later years.

1907

Joseph Rudyard Kipling

(December 30, 1865-January 18, 1936)

B. Bombay, India

D. Middlesex Hospital, London

English author, novelist, and journalist.

"in consideration of the power of observation, originality of imagination, virility of ideas and remarkable talent for narration which characterize the creation of this world-famous author"

He was educated in England, where he spent several unhappy childhood years later described in the short story Baa Baa, Black Sheep (1888) and in the autobiographical Something of Myself (1937). He gained a reputation as a humorist with The Village that Voted the Earth Was Flat (1913). His collection of verse, including Barrack-Room Ballads (1892), The Seven Seas (1896), and The Five Nations (1903), display a great range of technical achievement and a variety of subject matter. He was romantic in appearance and vigorous in language. According to Douglas Kerr " He is still an author who can inspire passionate disagreement and his place in literary and cultural history is far from over". He became a popular writer for children with the introduction of his character Mowgli, an East Indian boy brought up by a wolf pack. Around the turn of the century he was at the height of his fame, rich and admired, and still young. He detested publicity, despised popular applause, and ignored hostile criticism. He refused to be poet laureate and declined many public honors. He appears in the Jungle Book (1894), and the Second Jungle Book (1895). His first published book was a volume of poems, Departmental Ditties (1886).

Some other works: Captains Courageous (1897); The Man Who Would Be King (1888); Just So Stories (1902); The Day's Work (1898); Reward Fairies (1910); and Debits and Credits (1926).

1908

Rudolf Christoph Eucken

(January 5, 1846-September 15, 1926)

B. Aurich, Hanover, German Empire

D. Jena, Thuringia, Germany

German philosopher.

"in recognition of his earnest research for truth, his penetrating power of thought, his wide range of vision, and the warmth and strength in presentation with which in his numerous works he has vindicated and developed an idealistic philosophy of life"

He studied at Göttingen University. In 1871 he was appointed professor of philosophy at the University of Basel, Switzerland (1871-74), and at Gena University in Germany (1874-1920), and exchange professor at Harvard University (1912-13). He stressed the spiritual aspects of existence, and taught that people can by constant striving overcome the non-spiritual side of their nature. His books were inspirational and widely read. He believed that religious democracy, freedom, and international peace could be achieved only in a religious society based on spiritual autonomy. His philosophy was based around human experience, maintaining that humans have souls and that they are at the junction between nature and spirit. He believed that people should overcome their non-spiritual nature by continuous efforts to achieve a spiritual life. He gave considerable attention to social and educational problems. He delivered lectures in England in 1911 and spent 6 months in lecturing at Harvard University and elsewhere in the United States in 1912-13.

His works: The Problem of Human Life as Viewed by the Great Thinkers (1890); The Struggle for a Spiritual Content of Life (1896); The Truth of Religion (1901); Life's Basis and Life's Ideal (1907); The Meaning and Value of Life (1908); Main Currents of Modern Thought (1908); and Can We Still be Christians? (1911).

1909

Selma Ottilia Lovisa Lagerlöf

(November 20, 1858-March 16, 1940)

B. and D. Mårbacka, Wärmland, Sweden

Swedish author and short-story writer.

"in appreciation for the lofty idealism, vivid imagination and spiritual perception that characterize her writings"

She was the first woman to receive the Nobel Prize and in 1914 she became the first woman to be elected to the Swedish Academy. An early sickness left her lame in both legs, although she later recovered. She was a quiet child, more serious than others her age, with a deep love of reading. She had been writing poetry since she was a child, but she did not publish anything until 1890, when a Swedish Weekly gave her the first prize in a literary competition and published excerpts from the book which was to be her first, best, and most popular work. At the start of World War II, she sent her Nobel Prize Medal from the Swedish Academy to the Government of Finland to help raise money to fight the Soviet Union. After attending a teacher's seminary in Stockholm, Lagerlöf taught in a school in northern Sweden for 10 years. In 1895 she went to Italy on a traveling fellowship. A result of her trip was The Miracles of Anti-Christ (1897). The Wonderful Adventures of Nils (two volumes, 1906-7) describes in simple narrative form the folklore, geography, flowers, and animals of the various Swedish provinces. A 1900 visit to the American colony in Jerusalem became the inspiration for her book by that name. In 1895, she gave up her teaching to devote herself to her writing. In 1919 she sold all the movie rights to all of her as-yet unpublished works to Swedish Cinema Theatre.

Her works: Novels—Jerusalem (1901); The General's Ring (1925); Anna svärd (1928); Short stories: Invisible Links (1894); Märbacka (1922); Herr Arnes penningar (1903); Kökarlen (1912); and Troll och Människor (1915).

1910

Paul Johann Ludwig Von Heyse

(March 15, 1830-April 2, 1914)

B. Berlin, Germany

D. Munich, Germany

German prolific writer.

"as a tribute to the consummate artistry, permeated with idealism, which he has demonstrated during his long productive career as a lyric poet, dramatist, novelist, and writer of world-renowned short stories"

He studied Classical and Romance philosophy at the university of Berlin and Bonn. He often visited Italy, a country which inspired him throughout his life. He is best known today for his short stories (Novellas). He also wrote short stories and published several works, the most famous one is Kinder der Welt (Children of the World, 1873). In Berlin he was member of the poets' society Tunnel über der Speer in Munich. He wrote books, poems, and about 60 dramas. The sum of his many and varied productions made him a dominant figure among German men of letters (1855), which contained the popular L'Arrabbiata (The Fury), gained recognition for him throughout Germany. He is the fourth oldest laureates in literature, after Doris Lessing, Theodor Mommsen, and Jarslav Seifert. A street in Munich, 'Paul-Heyse Strasse' is made after him. His stories, though often lacking in depth, are polished in form. His translations from the Italian are recognized as outstanding achievements. Many of his works are psychological studies of the loves and conflicts of aristocratic characters. He published his first story, Jungbrunnen, in 1849, and devoted his life to the writing of verse tragedies, novellen, and poems. Among his best works are his translations of Giacomo Leopardi and other Italian and Spanish poets; many set to music by Hugo Wolf.

Other works: Merlin (1892); and Im paradiese (1875).

1911

Maurice Polydore Marie Bernard Count

Maeterlinck

(August 29, 1862-May 6, 1949)

B. Ghent, Belgium

D. Nice, France

Belgian playwright, poet and essayist who wrote in French. His plays form an important part of the Symbolist movement.

"in appreciation of his many-sided literary activities, and specially, of his dramatic works, which are distinguished by a wealth of imagination and by a poetic fancy, which reveals, sometimes in the guise of a fairy tale, a deep inspiration, while in a mysterious way they appeal to the readers' own feelings and stimulate their imaginations"

He was educated at Jesuit College and studied law, but a short practice as a lawyer in his home town convinced him he was unfit for the profession. He was drawn toward literature during a stay in Paris, where he associated with a number of men of letters and wrote his philosophical essays, plays, and verse influenced by French symbolists and he became the leading dramatist of the symbolist movement. He was predominantly a writer of lyrical dramas, but his first work was a collection of poems entitled Serres Chaudes (Hot Houses). It appeared in 1889, the same year in which his first play La Princesse Maleine, received enthusiastic praise from Octave Mirabeau, the literary critic of Le Figaro, and made him famous overnight.

Other works: Intruder (1890); The Blind (1890); Pelléas and Mélisande (1892); The Oiseau bleu (Blue Bird, 1809); La Vie des abeilles (The Lives of the Bee, 1901); La Mort de Tintagiles (The Death of Tintagiles, 1899); and Betrothal (1912). In 1948, the French Academy awarded him the Medal for the French Language.

1912

Gerhart Johann Robert Hauptmann

(Nov. 15, 1862-June 6, 1946)

B. Ober Salzbrunn, then Germany, now Poland

D. Agnetendorf, Poland

German preeminent novelist, dramatist, and poet.

"primarily in recognition of his fruitful, varied and outstanding production in the realm of dramatic art"

He is counted among the most important promoters of literary naturalism, though he integrated other styles into his work. The rapid advance in the physical and natural sciences demanded a reorientation and a new literary movement. Naturalism was in the making. Hauptman absorbed many of the new ideas, continued to read widely, attended scientific and historical lectures at the University of Berlin. Quite unexpectedly, and without much literary apprenticeship he achieved a tremendous success with Vor Sonnenaufgang (Before Sunrise, 1889). He studied at the academy of art in Breslau (1880-82) and turned to writing only after attempting to become a sculptor. He helped establish the naturalistic movement in German theatre with his early dramatic works. In the outstanding drama Die Weber (the Weavers, 1892), based on the revolt of Silesian weavers in 1844, the collective voices of the workers, rather than an individual, function as protagonist. He contributed two naturalistic stories, Fasching (1887) and Bahnwärter Thiel (1888), but achieved his first success with the play Before Dawn (1889). He was acclaimed during the period of Reimar Republic but largely disregarded by Nazi regime. He had three times received the highest Austrian drama award, the Grillparzer prize, in earlier years, and later the University of Leipzig (1909), the University of Prague (1921), and Columbia University (1932).

Some other works: Der Biberpelz (The Beaver Coat, 1893); Florian Geyer (1896); and Rose Bernd (1903).

1913

Sir Rabindranath Tagore (Thakur)

(May 7, 1861-August 7, 1941)

B. Calcutta, India

D. Calcutta, India

Bengali mystic, Brahmo poet, visual artist, playwright, novelist, and composer whose works reshaped Bengali literature and music in the late 19th century and early 20th century.

"because of his profoundly sensitive, fresh and beautiful verse, by which, with consummate skill, he has made his poetic thought, expressed in his own English words, a part of the literature of the West"

From 1878 to 1880 he studied law. He wrote 3000 poems, 2000 songs, 8 novels, 40 volumes of essays and short stories, and 50 plays. He drew inspiration both from his native Bengali and from English literature. He owed his formation as a writer to his education in the literatures of various languages: Sanskrit, his native Bengali, and English—thus combining the influences of classical and popular India with those of European culture. He was intensely aware of the wonder of creation and found in the Bengali landscape a lifelong source of inspiration. He was awarded Nobel Prize for his poetic work Gitanjali (song offerings, 1910). His efforts to combine Eastern and Western traditions brought him international acclaim. His major theme was humanity's search for God and truth. In 1980 he returned to India and saw the sufferings of the India's rural poor and grew to love the serenity of the Indian countryside. He was knighted in 1915. His profound symbolism, abetted by the free-flowing nature of his verse, create a universe of haunting beauty that express God's infinite love of humanity's deep compassion for all things beautiful.

Some of his works: Gora (Fair-Faced, 1910); Raja (The King of the Dark Chamber,1910); Visarjan (Sacrifice,1890); and Dak Ghar (The Post Office, 1912)

1915

Romain Rolland

(January 29, 1866-December 30, 1944)

B. Clamecy, Nièvre, France

D. Vézelay, France

French dramatist, essayist, art historian, mystic and pacifist.

"as a tribute to the lofty idealism of his literary production and to the sympathy and love of truth with which he has described different types of human beings"

Accepted to École normale supérieure in 1886, he first studied philosophy, but his independence of spirit led him to abandon that so as not to submit to the dominant ideology. He received his degree in history in 1889 and spent two years in Rome, where his discovery of Italian masterpieces were decisive for the development of his thought. When he returned to France in 1895, he received his doctoral degree. His best known work, the 10-volume novel cycle Jean-Christophe (1906-12) recounting the stormy career of a German musician, reflected his lifelong commitment to humanism. His wide cultural interests are illustrated not only by his studies of music and art but by his work toward a popular theatre and his plays on historical themes. He also wrote biographies of Beethoven (1903), Michelangelo (1908), and Tolstoy (1911). His pacifist stand during World War I aroused some hostility but made him a hero within the European intellectual community. A second novel cycle, The Soul Enchanted appeared between 1922-33. Never stopping his work, in 1940, he finished his memoirs. Shortly before his death, he wrote Péguy (1944), in which he examines religion and socialism through the context of his memoirs. Stefan Sweig, the Austrian writer, admired Rolland, when he once described him "the moral consciousness of Europe."

Some other works: Danton (1900); Le Quatorze Juillet (The 14th of July, Bastille Day, 1902); Robespierre (1938); and Le temps viendra (Time Will Come, 1903, drama).

1916

Carl Gustaf Verner von Heidenstam

(July 6, 1859-May 20, 1940)

B. Olshammar, Sweden

D. Övralid, Sweden

Swedish poet and novelist.

"in recognition of his significance as the leading representative of a new era in our literature"

He was a member of the Swedish Academy from 1912. Most of his works are passionate descriptions of the Swedish character. His poems and prose work are filled with a great joy of life, sometimes imbued with a love of Swedish history and scenery. He attended school in Stockholm, but his health was not good, and he went to Italy and the Orient and spent ten years abroad. Although he never studied at a university, he managed to acquire a good literary education through his own efforts. He also planned to make a career as an artist; his sense of color and his ability to see life with an artistic eye became a genuine asset for his poetry. He was a leader of the Neo-romantic movement. He returned to Sweden in 1887 and published his first volume of poetry Vallfart och vandringsår (Pilgrims: The Wander Years, 1888). He completely broke with the naturalistic school that then dominated Swedish literature. In colorful images, his verses celebrated the joy of life. His collected works were published in Stockholm in 15 volumes between 1909 and 1923.

His other works: Dikter (Poems, 1892); Karolinerna (The Charles Men, 2 volumes 1897-98); The Nya dikter (New Poems, 1915), deals with philosophical themes, mainly concerning the elevation of man to a better humanity from solitude; Et folk (1902); Skogen susar (The Forest Whispers, 1904); and Endymion (1889). His love of beauty is shown by the allegorical novel Hans Alienus (1892).

1917

Karl Adolph Gjellerup

(June 2, 1857-Oct. 13, 1919)

B. Roholte Vicarage at Praestø, Denmark

D. Klotzsche, Germany

Danish poet and novelist who together with his compatriot Henrik Pontoppidan won the Nobel Prize in Literature.

"for his varied and rich poetry, which is inspired by lofty ideals"

He was graduated from Haderslev Grammar School in 1874. He belonged to the Modern-Break-Through. He occasionally used pseudonym Epigonus. He was the son of a vicar in Zealand and grew up in a romantic idealistic atmosphere. In the 1870s he broke with his background and at first he became an enthusiastic supporter of the naturalist movement and Georg Brandes, writing audacious novels about free love and atheism. A central trace of his life was his Germanophobe attitude, he felt himself strongly attracted to German culture and in 1892 he finally settled in Germany. Among his works must be mentioned his most important novel Germannernes Laerling (The German Student, 1882). His other important novel Møllen (The Mill, 1896), is a sinister melodrama of love and jealousy. In his later years he was clearly influenced by Buddhism and Oriental culture. His work Der Pilger Kamanita (1906) has been called 'one of the oddest novels written in Danish.'

Other works: Den fuldendtes hustru (The Wife of the Perfect, 1907); Rudolph Stens Landpraksis (1913); and Das heiligste Tier (The Holiest Animal, 1919)).

His works have been translated into several languages, including German, Swedish, English, Dutch, Polish and others. The Pilgrim Kaminata is his most widely translated book, having been published in several European countries and America.

1917

Henrik Pontoppidan

(July 24, 1857-August 21, 1943)

B. Fredericia, Denmark

D. Ordrup, near Copenhagen, Denmark

He was the youngest, and perhaps the most influential members of the Modern-Break-Through. His works, typically written in a cold, aloof, epic style, present a comprehensive picture of his country and his epoch.

"for his authentic descriptions of present-day life in Denmark"

He intended to become an engineer, and for that purpose, studied at the Polytechnic Institute in Copenhagen. However, when he was 20, he decided to turn to writing as a profession. Noted for his mastery of style, he was essentially a naturalist who painted a stark and uncompromising picture of Danish people and society.

As a writer he was an interesting figure, distancing himself both from the conservative environment in which he was brought up and from his socialist contemporaries and friends. The first phase of his work continues rebellious social criticism. In matter-of-fact short stories he mercilessly describes the life of the peasants, with whom he lived in close contact. He was perhaps the first Danish progressive writer to break with an idealized portrayal of farmers. As a stylist he has been described as a born naturalist. His language looks plain, simple and easy but often loaded with symbols and secret hints, hidden irony and 'objective' descriptions. He is best known for three multi volume novels: Det forjaettede Land (The Enchanted Land, 1891-95), Lykke Per (Lucky Peter, 1898- 1904), and De dødes Rige (The Kingdom of the Dead, 1912-16).

Other works: Landsbybilleder (Village Pictures, 1883); Fra Hytterne (From the Cottages, 1887); Mands Himmerig (Man's Heaven, 1927); Nattevagt (Night Watch, 1894); And Den gamle Adam (Old Adam, 1894).

1919

Carl Friedrich Georg Spitteler

(April 24, 1845-December 29, 1924)

B. Liestal, Switzerland

D. Lucerne, Switzerland

Swiss poet of visionary imagination and author of pessimistic yet heroic verse.

"in special appreciation of his epic Olympian Spring"

From 1863 he studied law at the University of Zurich. From 1865 to 1870 he studied theology in the same institution, at Heidelberg and Basel. He worked in Russia as a tutor, starting in August 1871 until 1879. Later he was elementary teacher in Bern and Neuveville, as well as journalist for the Der Kunstwart and as editor for the Neue Zürcher Zeitung. In 1881 he published the allegoric Prose Prometheus and Epimetheus, published under the pseudonym Carl Felix Tandem. In 1900-1905 he wrote the allegoric-epic poem Olympischer Frühling (Olympic Spring). This work, mixing fantastic, naturalistic, religious and mythological themes, deals with human concern towards universe. Critics still consider Olympian Spring Spitteler's best and most important work. His prose work include Die Mädchenfeinde (Two Little Misogynists (1907), about his autobiographical childhood experiences, the dramatic Conrad der Leutnant (1898), in which he shows the influence from the previously opposed Naturalism, and the autobiographical novella Imago (1908), examining the role of unconscious in the conflict between creative mind and the middle-class restrictions. During World War I he opposed to the pro-German attitude of the Swiss-German speaking majority.

Other works: Gustav (1892); Balladen (1896); Der Parlamentär (1889); Lachende Wahrheiten (1898, essays); Glocken lieder (Grass and Bell Songs, 1906); and Imago (1906, a novel).

1920

Knut Hamsun Born: Knud Pendersen

(August 4, 1859-February 19, 1952)

B. Lom, Gudbrandsdal, Noerway

D. Grimstad, Nörholm, Norway

Norwegian poet, novelist, and dramatist.

Writing period (1877-1949).

"for his monumental work Growth of the Soil"

A pro-Nazi sympathizer, he was tried for treason after WWII, but it was escaped a prison sentence because of his advanced age. His first book appeared in 1877, but it was not until he had journeyed to the U.S. (1882-84, 1886-88), and had made his way to Copenhagen that he came to the attention of the literary world. His novel Sult (Hunger, 1890) was a sensation because of the revolutionary handling of its theme. He was considered by Isaac Bashevis Singer to be the 'father of modern literature.', and by King Haakon to be Norway's soul. He insisted that the intricacies of the human mind ought to be the main object of modern literature, to describe the 'whisper of the blood, and the pleading of the bone marrow.' He spent some years in America, traveling and working as a tram driver, and published his impressions, chiefly satirical, under the title Fra det moderne Amerikas Aandsliv (The Spiritual Life of Modern America). He first received wide acclaim with 1890 novel Sult (Hunger). A 15-volume of his complete works was published in 1954. In 2009, to mark the 150-year anniversary of his birth, a new 27-volume of his complete works was published, including short stories, poetry, plays, and articles, not included in the 1954 edition. Hamsun's works have been the basis of 25 films and television mini-series adaptations, starting in 1916.

Other works include Pan (1894); his best work, Markens Gröde (Growth of the Soil, 1917), an epic of the simple life, which won him the Nobel Prize.

1921

Anatole France (François-Anatole Thibault)

(April 16, 1844-Oct. 12, 1924)

B. Paris, France

D. Tours, France

French poet, journalist, critic, and a successful novelist with several best-sellers. Ironic and skeptical, he was considered in his day the ideal French man of letters.

"in recognition of his brilliant literary achievements, characterized as they are by a nobility of style, a profound human sympathy, grace, and a true Gallic temperament"

He was the most respected writer of his age by the time of his election to the Académie Française in 1896. For about 20 years he had several positions, but he always had enough time for his own writings. His literary output is vast, and though he is chiefly known as novelist and story teller, there is hardly a literary genre he did not touch upon at one time or another. He studied at the Collège Stanislas and after graduation he helped his father by working at his bookstore. In 1876 he was appointed a librarian for the French Senate. France had a brain just two-thirds the normal size, but this had no recorded effect on his life in any way. He wrote numerous books, including an early volume of poems in the Parnassian manner. Poèmes Dorés (1872); the successful novel The Crime of Sylvestere Bonnard (1881); At the Sign of the Reine Pédauque (1893); and an exquisite collection of short stories, The-Mother-of-Pearl Box (1892). His literary achievement was founded on his penetrating irony and his appreciation of classical art and 18th –century French literature.

Some other works: Penguin Island (1908), and his historical novel of French Revolution , Les Dieux ont soif (The Gods are Athirst, 1912); La Révolte des anges (The Revolt of the Angels, 1914); and Sur la Voie glorieuse (The Path of Glory, 1915).

1922

Jacinto Y Martínez Benavente

(Aug. 12, 1866-July 14, 1954)

B. Madrid, Spain

D. Madrid, Spain

One of the foremost Spanish dramatists of the 20th century. He returned drama to reality by way of social criticism.

"for the happy manner in which he has continued the illustrious traditions of the Spanish drama"

He never married. According to many sources, he was homosexual. He studied law, but when his father died and left him with a comfortable income, he abandoned his studies and traveled widely in France, England and Russia.

His major success in the theatre had for the most part been performed of nearly 170 plays of an outstanding variety of types which he continued to write and see performed through 1953, those of importance later than 1913 come perhaps to half a dozen. His forte is satire of society, subtle and ironic, the satire of the cynical, skeptical, sophisticated observer. He wrote for the love of theatre and it was by this work that he achieved honor and recognition in his native city and in theater capitals all over the world. A liberal monarchist and a critic of socialism, he was a reluctant supporter of Franco regime as the only viable alternative to what he considered the disastrous republican experiment of 1931-36. He published a collection of poems (1893) and achieved some fame with Cartas de mujeres (Women's Letters), a series of women's series, which was followed by another series in 1902. These letters gave him reputation as a brilliant stylist.

Other works: El nido ajeno (Another's Nests, 1894); Gente conocido (High Society, 1896); Señora ama (The Lady of the House, 1908); La malquerida (1913, drama); Tiatania (1946); and La infanzona (1947).

1923

William Butler Yeats

(June 13, 1865-January 28, 1939)

B. Sandymount, Dublin, Ireland

D. Roquebrune-Cap-Martin, France

Irish poet, dramatist, and prose writer.

"for his always inspired poetry, which in a highly artistic form gives expression to the spirit of a whole nation"

He was one of the foremost figures of the 20th century literature. He was educated in Dublin, Ireland, but spent his childhood in County Sligo. He studied poetry in his youth, and from his early age was fascinated by both Irish legends and occult. A pillar of both the Irish and British literature literary establishments, in his later years he served as a senator for two terms. He was a driving force behind the Irish literature Revival, and along with Lady Gregory founded the Abby Theatre, and served as its chief during its early years. He is generally considered one of the few writers whose greatest works were completed after being awarded the Nobel Prize whereas he received the prize chiefly for his dramatic works, his significance today rests on his lyric achievement. He wrote the introduction for Gitangali, which was about to be published by Indian Society.

His works: The Wild Swans at Coole (1919); Michael Robartes , Dancer (1921); The Tower (1928); The Winding Stair and Other Poems (1933); and Last Poems and Plays (1940) made him one of the outstanding and the most influential 20th-century poet writing in English. He was the leader of the Irish Literary Renaissance during the early 20th century. His early lyrical poetry and drama drew inspiration from Irish legend and occult learning. His recurrent theme are the contrast of art and life, masks, cynical theories of life and the ideal beauty and ceremony contrary with the hubbubs of modern life.

1924

Wladyslaw Stanislaw Reymont

(May 7, 1867-December 5, 1925)

B. Radomosko, Poland

D. Warsaw, Poland

Polish author whose work offers a vast panorama of Polish life in the last quarter of the 19th century.

"for his great national epic, The Peasants"

The Peasants, shows the author at the height of his powers and is a masterpiece of Polish literature. He was defiantly stubborn; after a few years of education in the local school he was sent to his father to Warsaw. He never completed schooling but was at various times in his youth a shop apprentice, a lay brother in a monastery, a railroad official, and an actor. Before adopting the career of a professional writer, he spent a restless early youth in a variety of occupations, and as a member of a traveling theatrical troupe he gained the first-hand knowledge of the theatre. His early writing includes Ziemia obiecana (The Promised Land 1899; filmed 1974), a story set in the rapidly expanding industrial town of Lódź and depicting the lives and psychology of the owners of the textile mills there. His two early novels Komediantka (The Comedienne, 1896) and Fermenty (The Ferments, 1897) were based on his own theatrical experience, while his short stories from peasant life show the strong influence of Naturalism. The novel Chtopi, 4 volumes (1904-09); The Peasants; filmed 1973), is a chronicle of peasant life during the four seasons of the year. Written almost entirely in peasant dialect, it has been translated into many languages. His later work was less expressive but reflected the variety of his interests, including his view of the spiritualist movement in Wampir (Vampire, 1911) and his image of Poland at the beginning of the partition process at the end of the 18th century.

1925

George Bernard Shaw

(July 26, 1856-November 2, 1950)

B. Dublin, Ireland

D. Hertfordshire, England

Irish playwright, critic, political activist, and social reformer.

"for his work which is marked by both idealism and humanity, its stimulating satire often being infused with a singular poetic beauty"

He authored more than 60 plays. He examined education, marriage, religion, government, health care, and class privilege and found them all defective. He was also awarded for writing Adapted Screen Play 'Pygmalion.'

He has been called the greatest dramatist in England since Shakespeare and the greatest British satirist since Jonathan Swift. He was a master of clear, direct prose.

His writings sparkle with wit and playfulness, but he was also capable of brutal irony. He attacked capitalism, militarism, hypocrisy, and the artificiality of moral and social conventions. He was one of the most influential music and drama critics of his time, a superb essayist, and a penetrating analyst of virtually every important aspect of Western culture—its economics, politics, and religion. Although his novels were ignored both by the critics and by the public, Shaw had begun to reach the public audience through his magazine articles—reviewing books for the Pal Mall Gazette. His first play Widowers' House was produced in 1892, followed rapidly by Philanderer (1893), and Mrs. Warren's Profession (1893).

Some of his other works: Arms and the Man (1894); Candida (1897); Caesar and Cleopatra (1899); Man and Superman (1905); Major Barbara (1907); My Fair Lady (1956); Back to Methuselah (1923); Saint John (1923); The Devil's Disciple (1897); Heartbreak House (1921); and The Apple Cart (1929).

1926

Grazia Deledda

(September 27, 1871-August 15, 1936)

B. Nuoro, Sardinia, Italy

D. Rome, Italy

Italian writer.

"for her idealistically inspired writings which with plastic clarity picture the life on her native island and with depth and sympathy deal with human problems in general"

She attended elementary school and then was educated by private tutor and moved to study literature on her own. She first published some novels on the magazine Lúltima moda. Nell`azzurro, published in 1890 might be considered her first work. Deledda's whole work is based on strong facts of love, pain and death upon which rests the feeling of sin and an inevitable fatality. In her novels there is always a strong connection between people, feelings and environment. Her novels depict vividly the life in Sardinia. Her literary skill was appeared at a very early age; when she was only 15, her first novel, Sangue Sardo was published. This and other early successes encouraged her to continue writing. She is notable for the lively descriptions of local background and for her understanding of psychology of the intense, rather simple Sardinians she portrays. Perhaps the greatest quality is the very simple but fundamental gift of good story-telling. She was widely regarded as Italy's greatest novelist. She placed less emphasis on local color and more on the religious and emotional elements that contribute to the dramatic vibrancy of her stories.

Her works: Il vecchio della montagna (The Old Man of the Mountain, 1900); Elias portolu (1903); Cerere (Ashes, 1904); La Madre (Mother, 1920); Dopo il divorzio (After the Divorce, 1902); and Cosima, an autobiographical novel, was published posthumously in 1937.

1927

Henri-Louis Bergson

(October 18, 1859-January 4, 1941)

B. Paris, France

D. Paris, France

French philosopher, influential in the first half of 20th century.

"in recognition of his rich and vitalizing ideas and the brilliant skill with which they have been presented"

He was internationally known for his concepts of inner duration, creative evolution, and limits of human intelligence. As a student he was tempted to pursue a career in mathematics; he was also a disciple of the mechanist Herbert Spencer. But by the time of his doctoral thesis, Time and Free Will (1889), Bergson had rejected the primacy of mathematical concept. When he was 18, he entered the famous École Normale Supérieure and obtained the degree of Licence-ès-Lettres, and this was followed by that of Agrégation de philosophie in 1881.After beginning his teaching career at Clermont-Ferrand in 1883, he joined the Collège de France (1900), where his lectures enjoyed unparalleled success until his retirement in 1921. In 1918 he was accepted into the French Academy. He emphasized the value of intuition in scientific thinking and argued that reality is beyond rational understanding. He had an acute, clear intelligence and fully appreciated the nature and value of science. Greater weight came to be attached to his philosophy after Einstein brought forward the theory of relativity, where time figured in a quite novel way. During World War II he participated in diplomatic missions designed to bring the U.S. into conflict.

Works: Matière et memoire (Matter and Memory, 1896); An Introduction to Metaphysics (1903); L' Evolution créatice (Creative Evolution (1907); The Two Sources of Morality and Religion (1932); and An Introduction to Metaphysics (1946).

1928

Sigrid Undset

(May 20, 1882-June 10, 1949)

B. Kalundborg, Denmark

D. Lillehammer, Denmark

Norwegian novelist.

"principally for her powerful descriptions of Northern life during the Middle Ages"

Having passed the intermediate exam; she took a one-year secretarial course and got a job as secretary with a major German-owned company in Kristyiana. She gained international fame as the author of historical novels. Her first novels were set in contemporary Norway. At the age of 25, Sigrid Undset made her literary debut with a short realistic novel on adultery, set against a contemporary background. Her best-known story of modern urban life is Jenny (1911); Images in a Mirror (1917) all deal with the role of modern women, caught between traditional duties and a new need for freedom. The historical trilogy Kristin Lavransdatter (The Wreath, The Wife, and The Cross, 1902) ranks as one of the great works of Norwegian literature. She converted to the Catholicism in 1925, and her historical novel, the tetralogy The Master of the Hestviken (The Axe, The Snake Pit, in the Wilderness, and The Son Avenger (1925-27), shows her preoccupation with religious questions. An early and forceful critic of Nazism, Undset fled to Sweden and then to the United States after the German invasion of Norway in 1945. A new period in the author's work began with a series of historical novels set in the Middle Ages. Her technique is distinguished by a straightforward, infinitely detailed, relentlessly honest description of man's character and circumstances, born of a passionate conviction. Sigrid Undset's home in Lillehammer, is now part of Maihaugen Museum.

Her other works: Olav Audunssøn (4 volumes, 1925-27); and Ida Elisabeth (1932).

1929

Paul Thomas Mann

(June 6, 1875-August 12, 1955)

B. Lübeck, Germany

D. Zürich, Switzerland

German novelist, short-story writer, social critic, philanthropist and essayist.

"principally for his great novel, Buddenbrooks, which has won steadily-increased recognition as one of the classic works of contemporary literature"

He is best known for his series of highly symbolic and ironic epic novels, and novellas, noted for their insight into the psychology of the artist and the intellectual. He attended the science division of Lübeck gymnasium, then spent time at the University of Munich and Technical University of Munich where, in preparation for journalism career, he studied history, economics, art history, and literature. He lived in Munich from 1891 until 1933, with the exception of a year in Palestrina and Italy. In his writings he sought to define enduring values and to show the importance of salvaging them from a decaying civilization. His first collection of short stories Little Herr Friedemann (1898), won critical acclaim. In stories of Three Decades, (1936), portrays the artist as an onlooker, or exile from society. In 1933 he emigrated to Switzerland, where he edited a periodical, Mass und Wert (Measures and Values, 1937-39), and then to the United States where he lived first in Princeton, New Jersey (1938-40) and then at Pacific Palisades, California.

Some of his other works: Königliche Hoheit (Royal Highness, 1916); Der Tod in Venedig (Death in Venice, 1924); Der Zauberberg (The Magic Mountain, 1927); Der Bajazzo (The Clown, 1897); Tonio Kröger (1903); A Gleam (1904); Dieser Friede (This Peace, 1838); Der Erwählte (The Holly Sinner, 1951); and Confessions of Felix Krull, Confidence Man (1954).

1930

Harry Sinclair Lewis

(February 7, 1885-January 10, 1951)

B. Sauk Centre, Minnesota, America

D. Rome, Italy

American novelist, short-story writer, and playwright.

He became the first American to be awarded the Nobel Prize.

"for his vigorous and graphic art of description and his ability to create, with wit and humor, new types of characters"

In late 1902, Lewis left home for a year at Oberlin Academy to qualify for acceptance by Yale University, where he got his bachelor's degree in 1908. His earliest published creative work—romantic poetry and short sketches—appeared in the Yale Courant and the Yale Literary Magazine; of which he became an editor.

He started his career as a free-lance journalist. His first success came with Main Street (1920). It was followed by another best-seller, Babbit, (a novel, 1922). His works are known for their insightful and critical views of American society and capitalist values, as well as their strong characterizations of modern working women. He achieved an international reputation in the 1920s for his satirical portrayal of middle-class life in Midwestern American small towns and cities in such novels as Main Street, Babbit, Arrowsmith, and Dodsworth (1929). As his biographer Mark Schorer wrote, the phenomenal success of Main Street "was the most sensational event in the 20th century American publishing history." He also won a Pulitzer Prize in 1926 for Arrowsmith, but he declined it.

Other works: Our Mr. Wrenn (1914); The Trail of the Hawk (1915); The Innocents (1917); Mantrap (1926); Ann Vikers (1933); Bethel Merriday (1940); The God-seeker (1949); It Can't Happen Here (1935); and World So Wide (1951).

1931

Erik Axel Karlfeldt

(July 20, 1864-April 8, 1931)

B. Karylbo, Dalarna, Sweden

D. Stockholm, Sweden

Swedish poet whose highly symbolist poetry masquerading as regionalism was popular and won him Nobel Prize posthumously in 1931; he had refused it in 1918. His strong ties to the peasant culture of his rural homeland remained a dominant influence on him all his life.

"the poetry of Erik Axel Karlfeldt"

Initially his name was Erik Axel Eriksson, but he assumed the new name in 1889, wanting to distance himself from his father who had suffered the disgrace of a criminal conviction. He studied at Uppsala University. After completing his studies, he held a position at the Royal Library of Sweden, and in Stockholm, for five years. In 1904 he was elected a member of the Swedish Academy.

In 1905 he was elected a member of the Nobel Institute of Academy, and in 1907, of Nobel Committee. In 1912 he was elected permanent secretary of the Academy, a position he held until his death. In 1917 he received an honorary doctorate from the University of Uppsala. His first collection Vildmarks-och Kärleksvisor (Songs of the Wilderness and of Love) was published in 1895. It was followed by Fridolins visor (Fridolin's Song, 1898), Fridolins lustgård (The Pleasure Garden, 1901), Flora och pomona (Flora and Pomona, 1906), and Hösthorn (The Horn of Autumn, 1927). A collection of his speeches appeared in print shortly after his death in 1931.

Selections of his poetry, translated into English by Charles Wharton Stork under the title Arcadia Borealis, were published in 1938.

Other works: Modern Swedish Poetry Part 1 (1929, translated by C.D. Locock); and The North! To the North (2001).

1932

John Glasworthy

(August 14, 1867-January 31, 1933)

B. Kingston Hill, Surrey, England

D. London, England

English novelist and playwright.

"for his distinguished art of narration which takes its highest form in The Forsyte Saga"

He was a dramatist of considerable skill. He was much admired for his serious examination of the inequalities of contemporary life. His critical look at the British legal system, The Silver Box (1907), was highly praised but failed to run despite the fine acting of his star, Ethel Barrymore. He attended Harrow and New College, Oxford, training as a barrister and was called to the bar in 1890 and 8 years later, after his first novel Jocelyn appeared he left law to continue writing. He was one of the most popular writers of the early 20th century. However, he was not keen to begin practicing law and instead traveled abroad to look after the family's shipping interests. During these travels he met Joseph Conrad, and the two future novelists became close friends. Four Winds was his first published work in 1897, a collection of short stories. These and several subsequent works, were published under the pen name John Sinjohn. His large Kingston upon Thames estate is now the site of three schools: Marymount International, Rokeby Preparatory School, and Holy Cross. The Silver Box (1906) became a success, and he followed it up with The Man of Property (1906). His plays addressed the class system and social issues, two of the best known being Strife (1909), and The Skin Game (1920).

Some other works: From the Four Winds (1897, as John Sinjohn); Fraternity (1909); The Little Dream (1911); Villa Ruebin (1900); A Man of Devon (1901); The Country House (1907); The Spirit of Punishment (1910); and The White Monkey (1924).

1933

Ivan Alekseyevich Bunin

(October 22, 1870-Nov. 8, 1953)

B. Voronezh, Russian Empire

D. Paris, France

Russian prose writer and poet.

"for the strict artistry with which he has carried on the classical Russian traditions in prose writing"

He was the first Russian to win the Nobel Prize for literature. The texture of his poems and stories sometimes referred to as 'Bunin Brocade', is one of the richest in the language. In the words of Soviet-era writer K.G. Paustovsky, the 1930 novel Life of Arseniev is an apical work of written Russian, but also one of the remarkable occurrences of world literature. He was sent to the public school in Yelets (Lipetskaya oblast) in 1881, but he had to return home in 5 years. He fled from Russia following the Revolution, and lived in Western Europe until his death.

At 17, he published his first poem in 1887 in a Saint Petersburg literary magazine. His first collection of poems Listopad (1901) was warmly welcomed by critics. In 1891 he published his first short story Country Sketch in literary journal. The best known of his translations is Longfellow's 'The Song of Hiawatha' for which he was awarded the Pushkin Prize in 1903. His first acclaimed novellas were On the Farm, The News from Home, To the Edge of the World and Other Short Stories (1897), Antonov Apples, and the Gentleman from San Francisco (1916), Brothers, Mitia's Love, The Affair of Cornet Yelagin. In 1930 he published two parts of a projected autobiographical trilogy: The Life of Arseniev, Temple of the Sun (1917), and Lika. He published his first full-length work, The Village, when he was 40 (1910-11). It was a bleak portrayal of village life, with its stupidity, brutality, and violence. In 1909, he was elected to Russian Academy.

1934

Luigi Priandello

(June 28, 1867-December 10, 1936)

B. Agrigento, Sicily, Italy

D. Rome, Italy

He was clearly the greatest playwright of his time, and has left a lasting mark on all the playwrights that have followed him.

"for his bold and ingenious revival of dramatic and scenic art"

He studied philology. From 1897 to 1922 he was professor of aesthetics and stylistics at Rome. By the age of 12 he had already written his first tragedy. At the insistence of his father, he was registered at a technical school, but eventually switched to the study of humanities at the Ginnasio, something which had always attracted him. His greatest achievement is in his plays. He wrote a large number of dramas which were published between 1918 and 1935, under the collective title of Maschere Nude (Naked Masks). In a play like se vi pare (Right You Are, If You Think You Are), two people hold contradictory notions about the identity of a third person. He wrote a great number of novellas which were collected under the title Novelle per un anno (Short Stories for a Year, 15 volumes , 1922-37). The attitudes expressed in L' Umorismo (Humor, 1908), are fundamental to all his plays. His characters attempt to fulfill their roles and are defeated by life itself which, always changing, enables them to see their perversity. Of his six novellas the best known are Il fu Mattia Pascal (The Late Mattia Pascal, 1904), and I vecchi e i giovani (The Old and the Young, 1913).

His works: Si gira (Shoot!, 1916); Uno, nessuno e Centomila (One, None, and a Hundred Thousand, 1926); Cestire gli ignudi (To Clothe the Naked, 1923); Enrico IV (Henry IV, 1922); and La vita che ti diedi (The Life I gave You (1924).

1936

Eugene Gladstone O'Neill

(October 16, 1888-November 27, 1953)

B. New York City, America

D. Boston, Massachusetts, America

He was a celebrated American playwright.

"for the power, honesty and deep felt-emotions of his dramatic works, which embody an original concept of tragedy"

His first published play Beyond the Horizon, was awarded the Nobel Prize. He was the son of James O'Neill, an actor famous for his role in The Count of Monte Cristo. He was sent to Catholic boarding school where he found his only solace in books. Many of his works, including The Iceman Cometh (1946) and Long Day's Journey into Night (1956), were made into films. Tennessee Williams observed: "O'Neill gave birth to the American theatre and died for it." During a lengthy artistic career (1913-43), he also won four Pulitzer Prizes—for Beyond the Horizon (1920), Anna Christie (1921), Strange Interlude (1928), and Long Day's Journey into Night (1956). He wrote only one well-known comedy (Ah, Wilderness!). Nearly all of his other plays involve some degree of tragedy and personal pessimism. He held up a mirror to American society and functioned as social critic and moral guide. After suffering from multiple health problems, O'Neill ultimately faced a severe Parkinson-like tremor in his hands which made it impossible for him to write. He died in Room 401 of the Sheridan Hotel on Bay State. As he was dying, he, in a barely audible whisper, spoke his last words: I knew it. I knew it. Born in a hotel room, and God damned it, died in a hotel room.

Some other works: Great God Brown (1926); Days Without End (1934); A Touch of the Poet (1957); More Stately Mansions (1962); Bound East for Cardiff (1916); Emperor Jones (1920); and The Hairy Ape (1922).

1937

Roger Martin du Gard

(March 23, 1881-August 22, 1958)

B. Neuilly-Sur-Seine, France

D. Bellême, France

French author who brought to his works a spirit of objectivity and a scrupulous regard for detail.

"for the artistic power of truth with which he has depicted human conflicts as well as some fundamental aspects of contemporary life in his novel-circle Les Thibault"

He attended two of the finest Paris lycees and, in 1906 graduated from the École des Charles with a thesis on an archaeological subject and with the degree of archivist-paleographer. After the years of the WWI, which he spent almost entirely in the front lines, he devoted most of his time to the writing of the roman-fleuvé. Les Thibault, which culminated in the three volume of L'Été (Summer, 1914). The twelve individual volumes of the series of novels appeared between 1922 and 1940. Les Thibault is a monumental picture of the world before the outbreak of World War I. Its rambling plot traces the history of Jacques Thibault, the rebel son of an upper middle-class family, against the background of the more staid destinies of his relatives. He first gained recognition with Jean Barrois (1913), a novel of France during the Dreyfus Affair. His fame, however, rests chiefly on the eight-part novel cycle The World of the Thibaults, a story of two families, one Roman Catholic and the other Protestant, it explores the conflicts of French society in the early 20th century.

Other works: Un Taciturne (The Silent One, 1932); Confidence africaine (African Secret, 1931); Vieille France (The Postman, 1933); Sur André Gide (Recollections of André Gide, 1913) appeared in 1951.

His complete work was published in two volumes in 1955.

1938

Pearl S. (Sydenstricker) Buck, also known as Sai Zhenzhu

(June 26, 1892-March 6, 1973)

B. Hillsboro, W Virginia, America

D. Danby, Vermont, America

American novelist. Her novel the Good Earth was the best- selling fiction in the U.S. in 1931 and won the Pulitzer Prize in 1932.

"for her rich and truly epic descriptions of peasant life in China for her biographical masterpieces"

She was raised in China and tutored by Confucian scholar Named Mr. Kung . She was taught English by her mother and her tutor. The Boxer Uprising greatly affected her and her family. In 1911, she left China once again for the United States to attend Randolph-Macon Woman's College, she would earn her degree (Phi Beta Kappa). She was an extremely passionate activist for human rights. She established Welcome House, Inc., the first international, interracial adoption agency. Her best known book, The Good Earth, was published in 1931. This became the best-selling of both 1931 and 1932, won Pulitzer Prize and The Howell's prize in 1935, and would be adapted as a major MGM film in 1937. In 1936, Buck wrote extremely successful twin biographies of her mother (The Exile) and her father (Fighting Angel: Portrait of a Soul). These moving account of their lives in China are largely credited with winning her the Nobel Prize. She was an indefatigable contributor to humanitarian causes, specially in behalf of orphaned Asian and retarded children. Her more than 85 works include many stories and journalistic pieces.

Some other works: East Wind, West Wind (1930); House Divided (1935); The Patriot (1939); The Big Wave (1948); The Hidden Flower (1952); Once Upon a Christmas (1972), Imperial Woman (1956); My Several Worlds (1954); and Death in the Castle (1965).

1939

Frans Eemil Sillanpää

(September 16, 1888-June 3, 1964)

B. Hämeenkyrö, Finland

D. Helsinki, Finland

Finnish writer. He was the foremost Finnish novelist of the first half of the 20th century.

"for his deep understanding of his country's peasantry and the exquisite art with which he has portrayed their way of life and their relationship with Nature"

His parents had experienced all the trials and tribulations common to generations of settlers in those parts of Finland. Frost had killed their seeds, farm animals had perished, and the farmer's children, too, had died, until only Frans Eemil, the youngest one, was left. He entered the University of Helsinki in 1908. At the university he devoted himself for some four years to natural sciences but took no degree. His debut as a novelist came in 1916, when Elämä ja Aurinko (Life and the Sun) was published. Much of his writing is colored by starkly realistic approach; he has been called the first social novelist of Finland. He won international fame for his novel Nuorena nukkunut (The Maid Silja Fallen Asleep While Young in 1931). The 23 years that separate the beginning and the apex of Sillanpää's career as a writer witnessed the appearance of a substantial number of novels and short stories. His novels have been translated into eighteen languages, including Hebrew and Japanese; he has enjoyed a particular vogue in Scandinavia, specially in Sweden. The University of Helsinki awarded him an honorary doctorate in 1936.

Some of his works: Hurkas Kurjuus (Meek Heritage, 1919); Hiltu ja Rangar (1923); Mann tasalta (From the Earth's Level, 1924); Rippa (Confession, 1928); Miehen tie (A Man's Way, 1932); and Virranpohjalta (From the Bottom of the Stream, 1933).

1944

Johannes Vilhelm Jensen

(January 20, 1873-November 25, 1950)

B. Farsøç, Jutland, Denmark

D. Copenhagen, Denmark

Danish author, often considered the first Danish writer of the 20th century.

"for the rare strength and fertility of his poetic imagination with which is combined an intellectual curiosity of wide scope and a bold, freshly creative style"

During half a century has endeavored to introduce the philosophy of evolution into the sphere of literature. He studied medicine in his youth, but he never practiced and turned to literature. In 1906 Jensen created his greatest literary achievement: the collection of Verses Digte (i.e. Poems 1906) His first two novels are Danskere (Dames, 1896) and Elkjaer (1898). His three volumes of Himmerlandshistorier (1898-1910) first brought him a measure of fame. In Kongens Fald (The Fall of the King, 1933) Jensen described the tragic life of King Christian II of Denmark. Like his compatriot Hans Christian Anderson, he traveled extensively, even to the United states. A poem of his, "Paa Memphis Station (At the Train Station, Memphis, Tennessee, U.S.A.) is well known in Denmark. The list of his work is very long, but it is generally conceded that superior to most of them are the six novels, daren (The Glacier), Det tabte Land (The Lost Country), Cimbrenes Tog, Skibet (The Ship), and Christopher Columbus. These works have been combined with two volumes as Den lange Rejse (The Long Journey, (1909-1920, 1922-1924). In them he begins with stories of the ancient martial Cimbrians of his native province of Himmerland and ends with a glowing tribute to Columbus and the New World; the story is intended to illustrate the irresistible progress of man through the ages.

1945

Gabriela Lucila Godoy Alcayaga Mistral

(April 7, 1889-January 10, 1957)

B. Vicuña, Chile

D. Hempstead, New York, U.S.A.

Chilean poet, educator, diplomat, and feminist who was the first Latin American to win the Nobel Prize.

"for her lyric poetry which, inspired by powerful emotions, has made her name a symbol of idealistic aspirations of the entire Latin-American world"

She enjoyed a continental reputation as a humanitarian and educator, and contributed greatly to post modernist verse. By age 15 she was supporting herself and her mother by working as a teacher's aide. An important moment of formal recognition came in December 22, 1914, when she was awarded first prize in a national literary contest Juegos Florales in Santiago with the work Sonetos de la Muerte (Sonnets of Death), which were inspired by a tragic love affair and grew into a large—and her best—collection, aptly entitled Desolación (Desolations, 1922). Her only other books of poetry are Ternura (Tenderness, 1924), Tula (Destruction, 1938), and Lagar (Winepress, 1954). Some central themes in her poems are nature, betrayal, love, a mother's love, sorrow and recovery, travel, and Latin American identity as formed from a mixture of Native American and European influences. Like many American artists and intellectuals, Mistral serves as a consul from 1932 until her death. "We are guilty of many errors and many faults, but our worst crime is abandoning the children, neglecting the foundation of life. Many of the things we need can wait. The child cannot. Right now is the time his bones are being formed, his blood is being made, and his senses are being developed. To him we cannot answer 'tomorrow,' his name is today."

Works: Tala (Harvesting, 1938); and Poema de Chile (Poem of Chile, (1967).

1946

Hermann Hesse

(July 2, 1877-August 9, 1962)

B. Claw , Würrtemberg, Germany

D. Montagnola, Switzerland

German-Swiss poet, novelist, and painter who had depicted in his work the duality of spirit and nature, body versus mind and the individual's spiritual search outside the restriction of society.

"for his inspired writings which, while growing into boldness and penetration, exemplify the classical humanitarian ideals and high qualities of style"

After a successful attendance at the Latin School in Göppingen, Hesse attended the Evangelist Theological Seminary in Maulbronn in 1891. At the end of 1892 he attended the Gymnasium in Cannstatt. In 1923 he received Swiss citizenship. He received the Goethe Prize of Frankfurt in 1946 and the peace prize of the German Booksellers in 1955. He also got Gottfried-Keller-Preis; and Honorary Doctorate from the University of Bern. Determined at the age of 13 "to be a poet or nothing" Hesse at first wrote derivative, romantic poems and stories of little merit. In his earliest novels, Peter Camenzind (1904) and Beneath the Wheel (1906) he won success. At the beginning of World War I, the strain of his pacific beliefs and domestic crises led him to undertake psychoanalysis with the follower of Carl Gustav Jung.

Jungian psychology gave his work a new dimension; Demian (1919), Siddhartha (1922), and Steppenwolf (1927) also reveal the influence of Nietzsche, Dostoyevsky, Spengler, and Buddhist mysticism.

His other works: Gertrude (1910); Klein und Wagner (1919); Siddhartha (1922); Narziss Und Goldmund (Death and the Lover, 1932); Journey to the East (1932); and Glass Bead Game (1943).

1947

André Paul Guillaume Gide

(Nov. 22, 1869-February 19, 1951)

B. Paris

D. Paris

French writer, humorist, and moralist.

"for his comprehensive and artistically significant writings, in which human problems and conditions have been presented with a fearless love of truth and keen psychological insight"

As a novelist, critic, and dramatist he addressed the problems and personal freedom within the confines of conventional moral and ethical codes. He went to become a champion of sincerity in all its forms, defending the right of each person to choose and to change his or her mind. He waged his war against conformity in prose pieces, in plays, and on the lecture platform. In his journals, plays, and miscellaneous pieces we encounter the rebel who believed in courage, fervor, and in individual freedom. He denounced political and social evil wherever he found it.

His career ranged in the symbolist movement, to the advent of anti-colonialism between the two World Wars. His first novel, Les d'André Walter, 1891 (The Notebooks of André Walters) was published when he was 22. In the same year he published Traité du Narcisse (The Treatise of the Narcissus). In 1924 he published an autobiography Si le grain ne meurt (If the Seed Dies). He left France for Africa in 1942 and lived in Tunis until the end of World War II. As the head of the eminent Nouvelle Revue Française (The New French Review), Gide fostered the best in French writing, publishing works by Proust, Cludel, Valéry, Giraudoux, and others who now rank with him as the great literary figures of the period.

His other works: Fruits of the Earth (1897); Lettres L'Immoraliste (The Immoralist (1902); Strait is the Gate (1909); Lafcadio's Adventures (1914); The Pastoral Symphony ((1919); and Counterfeiters (1925).

1948

T.S. Eliot (Thomas Stearns Eliot)

(September 26, 1888-January 4, 1965)

B. St. Louis, Missouri, U.S.A.

D. London, England

An Anglo-American poet, critic, dramatist, and editor. One of the most distinguished literary figures of the 20th century.

"for his outstanding, pioneer contribution to present-day poetry"

He was born in America and moved to England in 1914. Between 1906 and 1914 he attended Harvard, studying widely in literature and philosophy. As a graduate student in philosophy, Eliot went abroad to study principally at the Sorbonne and Oxford. In 1914, he decided to take up permanent residence in England and become a British citizen in 1927. He was influential in the modernist movement in poetry. He received wide recognition after the publication of The Waste Land (1922), which fused poetic traditions, posed moral questions, and combined disparate elements of modern music. Two years before The Waste Land appeared, Eliot's collection of essays on poetry and criticism, The Sacred Wood was published in 1920. With his best-known play, Murder in the Cathedral (1935) he hoped to revive poetic drama. After working as a philosophy assistant at Harvard from 1909 to 1910, Eliot moved to Paris, where from 1910 to 1911, he studied philosophy at Sorbonne. In 1927 he joined the Church of England. He was awarded the British Order of Merit in 1948 and the American Medal of Freedom in 1964. From 1920 to 1939 he edited The Criterion.

Other works: The Love Song of J. Alfred Prufrock (1909-11); Portrait of a Lady (1915); The six-part poem Ash Wednesday (1930); The Family Reunion (1939); The Cocktail Party (1949); The Confidential Clerk (1953); and The Elder Statesman (1959).

1949

William Cuthbert Faulkner

(September 25, 1897-July 6, 1962)

B. New Albany, Mississippi, U.S.A.

D. Byhalia, Mississippi, U.S.A.

He was one of America's most innovative novelists.

"for his powerful and artistically unique contribution to the modern American novel"

His reputation is based on his novels, novellas and short stories. He is also a published author and occasional screenwriter. He is now deemed the greatest American writers of all times. He attended the University of Mississippi from 1919 to 1921. His works combined regional traditions and cultures with masterly characterization and technical experimentation. In a career of more than three decades he published 19 novels, and more than 80 short stories. He portrayed the decadence of the South in many of his novels and short stories. The Sound and the Fury (1929) and Sanctuary (1931) won him a place among the major figures of contemporary American literature. He was elected to the American Academy of Arts and Letters in 1948. A voracious reader, he began writing in his early teens. As a young man he produced hand-lettered and hand-illustrated books for his friends. In his Nobel Prize acceptance speech, Faulkner summed up a lifetime of writing: "The poet's voice need not merely be the record of man, if can be one of the props, the pillars to help him endure and prevail." The Bear. A Fable (1954) and The Reivers (1962) each won Pulitzer Prize for fiction. He donated part of his Nobel money 'to establish a fund to support and encourage new fiction writers'.

Other works: A volume of poetry The Marble Faun (1924); Dr. Martino (1934); Knight's Gambit (1949); and the novels As I Lay Dying (1930), Light in August (1932), Absalom, Absalom! (1936), The Hamlet (1940), and Go Down, Moses (1942).

1950

Bertrand Arthur William Russell

3rd Earl, Russell

(May 18, 1872-Feb. 2, 1970)

B. Trelleck, Monmouthshire, England

D. Penrhyndeudraeth, Wales, England

British philosopher, historian, advocate for social reform, and mathematician.

"in recognition of his varied and significant writings in which he champions humanitarian ideals and freedom of thought"

He was the grandson of the 1st Earl Russell, who had twice been the prime minister of Great Britain. He is considered one of the founders of analytic philosophy. He made major contributions in the areas of mathematics, logic, education, and social reform. He was educated at Trinity College, Cambridge University, and remained there as a fellow (1895-1901) and lecturer (1910-16). He took an active interest in moral, educational, and religious issues. He traveled, wrote, and lectured widely in Great Britain and America in the interwar period. He found the Campaign for Nuclear Disarmament (1958) and the Committee of 100 (1960) as his advocacy of civil disobedience progressively stronger than the antinuclear movement. His reviews, as set forth in his book Why I Am Not a Christian (1927), were considered controversial by many. He remained active and wrote extensively until his death at 97. While ranging over an immense field, Russell demonstrated an openness of ideas, an aversion to dogma, and a rigor in analysis that more than justify as a fountainhead of 20th century English and American.

His works: Our Knowledge of the External World (1914); Analysis of Mind (1921); The ABC of Atoms (1923); The ABC of Relativity (1923); Education and the Good Life (1926); Special Essays (1928); Marriage and Morals (1929); and The Conquest of Happiness (1930).

1951

Pär Fabian Lagerkvist

(May 23, 1891-July 11, 1974)

B. Växjö, Sweden

D. Stockholm, Sweden

Swedish poet. He wrote poems, plays, novels, stories, and essays of considerable expressive power and influence from his early 20s to his late 70s.

"for the artistic vigor and true independence of mind with which he endeavors in his poetry to find answers to the eternal questions confronting mankind"

He received a traditional religious education which strongly influenced all his works. When he visited Paris in 1913, he was attracted to intellectual movements in art that were alien to his religious and traditional upbringing. Among his central themes was the fundamental question of good and evil. As a moralist, he used religious motifs and figures from the Christian tradition without following the doctrines of the church. His pessimism about human nature and the individual's place in a meaningless world deepened during World War I. He protested against the brutality in the world in the novel The Hangman (1933), The Dwarf (1944), and The Barabbas (1950) were studies of the struggle between good and evil inherent in the human condition.

One of the author's earliest work is Angest (Anguish, 1916), a violent and disillusioned collection of poems. His anguish was derived from his fear of death, the World War, and a personal crisis. "Anguish, anguish is my heritage/ the wound of my throat/the cry of my heart in the world."

His works: Sista Människan (The last Man, 1917); The Secret of Heaven (1919); Det eviga leendet, three stories (The Eternal Smile, 1920); Den lyckliges väg (The Happy Man's Way, 1921); Guest of Reality (1925); Devärgen (The Dwarf, 1944); Aftonland (Evening Land, 1953); and The Sibyl (1956).

1952

François Charles Mauriac

(October 11, 1885-September 1, 1970)

B. Bordeaux, France

D. Paris, France

French author, novelist, playwright, essayist, poet, and journalist, member of Académie française (1933). He was also awarded the Grand Cross of the Légion d'honneur in 1958. Though Mauriac's fame outside France spread slowly, he was regarded my many as the greatest French novelist after Marcel Proust.

"for the deep spiritual insight and the artistic intensity with which he has in his novels penetrated the drama of human life"

He is acknowledged to be one of the greatest Roman Catholic writers of the 20th century. He studied at the University of Bordeaux, graduating in 1950, after which he moved to Paris to prepare for postgraduate study at the École des Charles. He was opposed to the rule in Vietnam, and strongly condemned the use of torture by the French army in Algeria. He also published a series of personal memoirs and a biography of Charles de Gaule. His novels are set among middle-class people in his native Bordeaux. The attitudes toward sin and love expressed in his fiction reflects his Roman Catholic faith. His novels explore the mysteries of human existence, the nature of destiny, and the human guilt before a judging though forgiving God.

His stories are noted for their psychology and beautiful language. In 1934 he began to write essays on view of life and literature for the newspaper Le Figaro.

Other works: Le Désert de l'amour (The Desert of Love, 1925); Thérèse (1927); Vipers' Tangle (1932); A Woman of Pharisees (1941); God a Mammon (1927); Asmodée (1938). And the two interesting autobiographical works, the 5-volume journal (1934-53) and Mémoires Intérieures (1959).

1953

Sir Winston Leonard Spencer Churchill

(November 30, 1874-January 24, 1965)

B. Blenheim, Oxfordshire, England

D. Hyde Park, London, England

British politician known chiefly for his leadership of the United Kingdom from 1940-45 and 1951-55.

"for his mastery of historical and biographical description as well as for brilliant oratory in defending exalted human values"

After failing entrance exams he was finally admitted to the Royal Military College at Sandhurst. He was elected to the House of Commons in 1900. He rallied Britain and the forces of freedom everywhere with his indomitable spirit and rugged oratory. He became a familiar figure to millions with his bulldog expression, huge cigar, and two fingers held high in a V-for-victory sign. One of his greatest weapon was his oratory. "I have nothing to offer but blood, toil, tears, and sweat." He told the Commons on taking office. He is the only British Prime Minister who has ever received the Nobel Prize in Literature and the only second person to be made an Honorary Citizen of the United States. He was the Prime Minister of England from 1940 to 45 and 1951 to 55. At the forefront of the political scene for almost 50 years, he held many political and cabinet positions. Before the World War I, he served as President of the Board of Trade, Home Secretary, and First Lord of the Admiralty. His major work, the biography of his father Lord Randolph Churchill was published in 1906. His other famous biography, the life of his great ancestor, the Duke of Marlborough, was published in four volumes between 1933 and 1938. His History of the World War I and World War II ran to six volumes (1948-1953/54). His magnificent oratory survives in 12 volumes of speeches, among them The Unrelenting Struggle (1942); The Dawn of Liberation (1945); and Victory (1946).

1954

Ernest Miller Hemingway

(July 21, 1899-July 2, 1961)

B. Oak Park, Illinois, U.S.A.

D. Ketchum, Idaho, U.S.A.

American novelist, short-story writer, and journalist.

"for his mastery of the art of narrative, most recently demonstrated in The Old Man and the Sea, and for the influence that he has exerted on contemporary style"

He was part of the 1920s expatriate community in Paris. He also received the Pulitzer Prize for The Old Man and the Sea. He was the foremost spokesman for the "Lost Generation" of young intellectuals who were disillusioned and embittered by World War I. His talent for understatement, for making simple but strong words suggest more than they actually say, inspired many writers to imitate him. He often depicts primitive 'human' types who are defeated in courageous battles against nature or fate. Hemingway attended Oak and Park and River Forest High School from September 1913 until graduation in June 1917. He excelled both academically and athletically; he boxed, played American football, and displayed particular talent in English classes. After graduation from high school, he was a reporter on the Kansas City Star. He was also a newspaper correspondent in the Spanish Civil War and World War II. In 1959 he bought a house in Ketchum, Idaho, where he committed suicide in the summer of 1961.

Other works: Men Without Women (1927); The Snows of Klimanjaro and The Short Happy Life of Francis Macomber (1938); The Sun Also Rises (1926); A Farewell to the Arms (1929); To Have and Have Not (1937); Three Stories and Ten Poems (1923); and For Whom the Bell Tolls (1940).

He was awarded silver medal of Military Valor in World War I and American Academy of Arts and Letters Award of Merits, 1954.

1955

Halldór Kiljan Laxness

(April 23, 1902-February 8, 1998)

B. Rekjavik, Iceland (Capital of Iceland)

D. Reykjavik, Iceland

20th century Icelandic and author of Independent People (1934-35), The Atom Station (1948), and Iceland's Bell (1943-46).

"for his vivid epic power which has renewed the great narrative art of Iceland"

In 1922, laxness joined the Abbaye St. Maurice et St. Maur in Clervaux in Luxembourg, where he practiced self-study, read books, and studied French, Latin, theology and philosophy. While there, he also composed the story Undir helgahnúk (Under the Holy Peak) in 1924. During his career he wrote poetry, newspaper articles, plays, short stories, and fifteen novels. The chaos of Germany affected him deeply, following the example of the Danish poet Johannes Jörjensen, he turned Catholic in 1923. He turned to socialism, an ideology that is reflected in his novels written in the 1930s and 1940s. At the age of 17, he traveled to Europe, where he spent several years. He is considered the most creative Icelandic writer of the 20th century. His first novel, Vefarinn mikli frá kashmír (The Great Weaver from Kashmir, 1927), is about a young man who is torn between his religious faith and the pleasures of the world. He also wrote an autobiography entitled Skáldatími (A writer's Schooling, 1963) and a documentary novel entitled Innansveitarkronika (Parish Chronicle, 1970).

Some other works: Salka Valka (part I, 1931); Salka Valka (part II, 1932); Heiman eg fór (1952); The Fish Can Sing (1957); Gerpla (Happy Warriors, 1952); Nokkrar sögur (1923); Fötatak manna (1933); and Shaumorf (1934).

In 1953 Laxness was awarded the Soviet-sponsored World Peace Council Literary Prize.

1956

Juan Ramón Jiménez Mantecón

(December 24, 1881-May 29, 1958)

B. Monguer, Andalusia, Spain

D. Santruce, Puerto Rico

Spanish poet, a prolific writer.

"for his lyrical poetry, which in Spanish language constitutes an example of high spirit and artistical purity"

One of his most important contributions to modern poetry was his advocacy of the French concept of "pure". He studied in the Jesuit College in Puerto de Santa Mariá and in 1896 entered the University of Seville but soon abandoned academic studies and began to write for newspapers. In 1936 he left Spain for America, and established residence finally in Puerto Rico.

His works can be divided into three periods: the period of his beginning efforts (1898-1904), and the period of modernist influence (1905-1915), and the period of maturity (after 1915).

His first work was a book of verse, Rimus (1902), which was followed by Arias tristes (1903), and Jardines lejanos (Distant Gardens, 1904). He first produced several volumes of verse that identified him with the Spanish modernist movement. His Almas de Violeta (Violet Souls, 1900); Ninfeas (Water Lilies, 1900); Airas tristes (Sad Airs, 1903), display the preoccupation with love, natural beauty, and death that would also haunt his later work. His subsequent volumes, illustrating both his denuded style and a growing mysticism, include Enternidades (Eternities, 1918); Piedra y cielo (Stone and Sky, 1919); La estación total (All seasons in One, 1946); and Animal de fondo (Animal of the Depths, 1949). He also wrote the personal sketches collected in the Españoles deters mundos (Spaniards of three Worlds, 1942); and translated Blake, Eliot, and Rabindranath Tagore (with his American-born wife). He left Spain during the Spanish Civil War.

1957

Albert Camus

(November 7, 1913-January 6, 1960)

B. Montovi, Algeria

D. Villeblevin, France

Algerian-born French author, philosopher, and journalist.

"for his important literary production, which with clear-sighted earnestness illuminates the problems of the human conscience in our times"

Through his writings, and in some measure, he became the leading moral voice of his generation during the 1950s. At the height of his fame, Camus died in a car accident, only three years after receiving the award. Although born in extreme poverty, Camus attended the lycée and university in Algiers, where he developed an abiding interest in sports and the theatre. His university career was cut short by a severe attack of tuberculosis, an illness from which he suffered throughout his life. Camus is unquestionably one of the most significant authors of the mid-20th century and his influence has been worldwide. He was a gifted writer, deeply sensitive to the beauty of the Mediterranean world, with its light, sea, and bare hills; his works are rich in an imagery from the natural landscapes he loved. Because of his origins he felt a deep blend of solidarity with the great masses of human beings who suffered so greatly from the political upheavals and murderous wars of the century. The themes of poverty, sport, and horror of human mortality all figure prominently in his volumes of so-called Algerian essays: L' Envers et l' Endroit (The Wrong Side and the Right Side, 1937), Noces (Nuptials, 1938), and L' Été (Summer, 1954). His views contributed to the rise of philosophy known as Absurdism.

Other works: L' Etranger (The Stranger, 1942); La Peste (The Plague, 1947); La Chute (the Fall, 1957); Caligula (1944); L' Etat de Siège (State of the Siege, 1948); and Les Justes (The Just Assassins, 1949).

1958

Boris Leonidovich Pasternak

(February 10, 1890-May 30, 1960)

B. Moscow, Russia

D. Peredelkino, Russia

Russian poet and writer.

"for his important achievement both in contemporary lyrical poetry and in the field of the great Russian epic tradition"

In the west he is best known for his epic novel Dr. Zhivago, a tragedy whose events span the last period of Transit of Russia, and the early days of the Soviet Union. My Sister, Life, written in 1922, is arguably the most influential collection of poetry published in the Russian language in the 20th century. Reluctant to publish his own poetry, he turned to translating Shakespeare, Goethe, Rilke, Paul Verlaine, and Georgian poets. Inspired by one of his neighbors, Pasternak resolved to become a composer and entered the Moscow Conservatory. In 1910 he abruptly left the conservatory for the University of Marburg, where he studied under Neo-Kantian philosopher Hermann Cohen and Nicolai Hartmann. Although invited to become a scholar, he decided against making philosophy a profession and returned to Moscow in 1914. He won international recognition as a major novelist, although he was much criticized in his native Russia. Many of his poems and some of his prose works have strong religious overtones.

In his prose and verse, human lives are shaped primarily by love, faith, and destiny. Dr. Zhivago was rejected by Soviet publishers as anti Soviet. It was smuggled to the West by an Italian Communist publisher and was soon printed in many languages.

His works: A Twin in the Clouds, 1914; Leytenant Shmidt (Lieutenant Schmidt, 1927); Vtoroye rozhdenie (The Second Birth, 1932); Over the Barriors (1916); Safe Conduct (1931); and Over the Barriors (1916).

1959

Salvatore Quasimodo

Pen name: Salvatore Ragusa

(August 20, 1901-June 14, 1968)

B. Modica, Sicily, Italy

D. Naples, Italy

Italian author.

"for his lyrical poetry, which with classical fire expresses the tragic experience of life in our own times"

Along with Giuseppe and Eugenio Montale, he is one of the foremost Italian poets of the 20th century. In 1919 he graduated in the local Technical College. In 1917 he founded the short-lived Nuovo giornale letterario (New Literary Journal) in which he published his first poems. In 1919 he moved to Rome to finish his engineering studies, at the same time he studied Greek and Latin. In 1934 he moved to Milan. Starting from 1938 he devoted himself entirely to writing. In 1938 he became professor of Italian literature at the Conservatory of Music in Milan, a city he had already made his home. He published his first collection, Acque de terre (Waters and Lands) in 1930. In 1932 he published a new collection Òboe sommerso (Sunken Oboe) including all his lyrics from 1930-32. In 1931 he was transferred to Imperia and then to Genoa where he got acquainted with Camillo Sbarbaro and other personalities of the Circoli magazine, with which Quasimodo started a prolific collaboration. In 1938 he published Poesie, followed the translations of Lirici greci (Greek Lyrics) in 1939. In his last years he made numerous voyages in Europe and America, holding public speeches and public lectures. Though an outspoken anti-Fascist, during World War II he did not take part in the Italian resistance against the German occupation. In that period he devoted himself to the translation of the Gospel of John, of some of catullus's cantos, and several episodes of the Odyssey.

1960

Saint-John Perse (Alexis Leger)

(May 31, 1887-September 20, 1975)

B. Pointe-à-Pitre, Guadeloupe

D. Provence, France

French poet and diplomat

"for the soaring flight of the evocative imagery of his poetry which in a visionary fashion reflects the conditions of our time"

The son of a lawyer, he received his higher education in France. He studied at Bordeaux and after private studies in political science went into the diplomatic service in 1914. He frequented cultural clubs where he met Paul Claudel and Oclidon Redon. He wrote poems inspired by the story of Robinson Crusoe and undertook a translation of Pindar. By 1933 he had reached the highest permanent post in the service—secretary of the foreign ministry remaining in this post through cabinet changes of the 3rd Republican, he fell under the violent attack of the Vichy regime in 1940, was deprived of his citizenship and possessions, and fled to the United States, where he served as a consultant to the Library of Congress. There he had a brilliant career.

During his American exile, wrote his long poems Exil, Vents, Pluies, Amers, and Chroniques. In 1924 he published Anabase, using the pseudonym of Saint-John Perse for the first time. He held successive important positions within the foreign office. He declined a teaching position at Harvard University, preferring to focus on his writings. As his diplomatic career ceased, his career in poetry flowered anew. His works have been translated by famous poets into many languages.

His works: Èloges (1911); Pluies (1943); Neiges (1944); Chronique (1960); Poesie (1961); Oiseaux (1963); Pour Dante (1965); Noctume (1973); and Sécheresse (1973).

Before his death, Leger donated his library, manuscripts and private papers to Foundation Saint-John Perse.

1961

Ivan (Ivo) Andrić

(October 9, 1892-March 13, 1975)

B. Dolac (village near Travnik), Bosnia

D. Belgrade, Serbia

Serbo-Croation novelist and short-story writer. His literary career spanned some 60 years.

"for the epic force with which he has traced themes and depicted human destinies drawn from the history of his country"

Originally named Ivan, he became known the diminutive Ivo. He attended the Jesuit gymnasium in Travnik, followed by Sarajevo's gymnasium and later universities in Zagreb, Vienna, Kraców, and Graz. Because of his political activities, Andrić was imprisoned by the Austrian government. During World War I. Under the newly-formed Kingdom of the Serbs, Croats, and Slovenes. He became a civil servant, first in the Ministry of Faiths and then the Ministry of Foreign Affairs. The works of Ivo Andrić particularly his thesis 'The Development of Spiritual Life in Bosnia under the influence of Turkish Rule' has resurfaced as source of anti-Muslim prejudice in Serbian cultural discourse. He pursued a successful diplomatic career, as Deputy Foreign Minister and later ambassador to Germany. He was also a delegate of the Kingdom of Yugoslavia at the 19th, 21st, 23rd and 24th session of the League of Nations. During World War II, Andrić lived quietly in Belgrade, completing his most famous novels which were published in 1945, including The Bridge on the Drina. He donated all the prize money for the improvement of the libraries in Bosnia and Herzegovina.

Other works: Bosnian Chronicle (1945); The Woman from Sarajevo (1945); Ex Ponto (1918); Unrest (Nemiri, 1920); The Damned Yard (Prokleta Avlija, 1945); and Omer-Pasha Latas (posthumously in 1977).

1962

John Ernst Steinbeck, Jr.

(February 27, 1902-December 20, 1968)

B. Salinas Valley, California, U.S.A.

D. New York City, U.S.A.

American author and writer. He wrote the Pulitzer Prize-winning novel The Grapes of Wrath in 1939 and the novella Of Mice and Men in 1937.

"for his realistic and imaginative writings, combining as they do sympathetic humor and keen social perception"

He based all his novels on the American experience, often with sympathetic focus on the poor, the eccentric, or the dispossessed. Form 1919 to 1925 he studied intermittently at Oxford University but did not receive a degree. He was of German and Irish descent. During World War II, he served as a war correspondent for the New York Herald Tribune and worked for the Office of Strategic Services. His early novels Cup of Gold (1929), The Pastures of Heaven (1932), and To a God Unknown (1933), aroused little public interest. He turned to filmmaking after the film success of The Grapes of Wrath. He wrote impressive screenplays for the Mexican-based The Forgotten Village (1941), and Viva Zapata (1938), as well film scripts for his stories The Red Pony (1938) and The Pearl (1947). He devoted several years to his most ambitious project, East of Eden (1952). He wrote popular sketches on his travels in Once There Was a War (1958), Travels with Charles (1962), and America and Americans (1966). In all, he wrote 27 books, including 16 novels, six non-fiction books and several collections of short stories. In 1948 he toured the Soviet Union with renowned photographer Robert Capa. They visited Moscow, Kiev, Tbilisi, Batumi and Stalingrad. His book about their experiences, A Russian Journal, was illustrated with Capa's photos.

Other works: Cannery Row (1945); The Wayward Bus (1947); and The Winter of Our Discontent (1961).

1963

Giorgos (George) Seferis

(Pen name for Georgis Seferidas).

(March 13, 1900-September 20, 1971)

B. Urla, Smyrna Asia Minor, Ottoman Empire

D. Athens, Greece

One of the most important Greek poets of the 20th century.

"for his eminent lyrical writing, inspired by a deep feeling for the Hellenic world of culture"

Having fled (1914) with his family from Turkish-dominated Smyrna to Athens, he studied there and in Paris, becoming a lawyer and diplomat. He continued his studies in Paris from 1918 to 1925, studying law at Sorbonne. While he was there, in September 1922, Smyrna was captured by Turks after a two year Greek occupation and its Greek population, including Seferis' family fled. He returned to Athens in 1925 and was admitted to the Royal Greek Ministry of Foreign Affairs in the following year. This was the beginning of a long and successful career, during which he held posts in England (1931-34), and Albania (1936-38). During the Second World War, Seferis accompanied the Free Greek Government in exile to Crete, Egypt, South Africa, and Italy and returned to the liberated Athens in 1944. He was appointed minister to Lebanon, Syria, Jordan, and Iraq (1953-56). Influenced by T.S. Eliot, whose poetry he translated into Greek, Seferis became the leading member of the Generation of 1930 through his superbly crafted poems and essays on poetry. Among his Collection Poems (1924-55), Mythistorima (1935) depicts the spiritual emptiness of contemporary life through the evocation of ancient mythology. The Thrush (1946) employs mythology to express feeling of uprooting and exile. He also published Three Secret Poems (1966) and an essay collection, On the Greek Style (1966).

Works: Antigrafes (Translations, 1965) and Tria Kryfa Poiimata (The Secret Poems, 1966).

1964

Jean-Paul Charles Aymard Sartre

(June 21, 1905-April 15, 1980)

B. Paris

D. Paris

French leading existentialist, lawyer, novelist, screen writer, political activist, biographer, and literary critic.

"for his works which, rich in ideals and filled with the spirit of freedom and the quest for truth, has exerted a far-reaching influence on our age" (He declined the prize).

He graduated from the École Normal Supérieure, Paris, in 1929, by which time he had met Simone de Beauvoir, who became his lifelong companion as well as his intellectual associate. Since 1945 he developed himself exclusively to writing and editing the journal Les Tempes Modernes (Modern Times). He spent a year as a prisoner of war during World War II and was a key figure among the French intellectuals who resisted the Nazi occupation. He presented his philosophical theories in novels, plays, short stories, treatises, and essays. He studied philosophy in France and Germany, and taught philosophy in France for several years. He fought in World War II, was captured by Germans in 1940, and was released nine months later. His work has also influenced sociology, critical theory, post-colonial theory, and literary studies, and continues to influence these disciplines. His philosophical ideas are elaborated in such treatises as Being and Nothingness (1943), and Existentialism is a Humanism (1946). Among his best works from a literary standpoint are his first novel, Nausea (1938); a play, The Flies (1943); and The Words (1963). .

Selected works: No Exit (1944); The Respectful Prostitute (1946); The Devil and the Good (1951); The Condemned of Altona (1959); Collection of Essays—Between Existentialism; Marxism (1975); Reprieve (1945); and The Roads to Freedom (1945-49).

1965

Mikhail Alexandrovich Sholokhov

(May 24, 1905-February 21, 1984)

B. Veshenskaya, Russian Empire

D. Veshenskaya, USSR

Soviet- Russian novelist and short-story writer.

"for the artistic power and integrity with which, in his epic of the Don, he has given expression to a historic phase in the life of the Russian people"

During the civil war he was on the side of the revolutionaries and in 1922 he went to Moscow to be a Journalist. He attended schools in Kargin, Moscow, Boguchar, and Veshenskaya until 1918, when he joined the revolutionary side in the Russian civil war at the tender age of 13. He began writing at 17. He completed his first literary work, the short story, the Birthmark, at 19. After going to the Red Army in 1920 and spending two years in Moscow, he returned to his native Cossack village in the Don region in 1924. He made several trips to Western Europe and in 1959 accompanied Khrushchev to the United Nations. His most controversial work Tikhii Don, (The Silent Don) is remarkable for the objectivity of its portrayal of the heroic and tragic struggle the Don Cossacks against the Bolsheviks for independence. It took him twelve years to publish it (4 volumes, 1928-40). His first book Tales from the Don, a volume of his native region during World War I and The Russian Civil War, largely on his personal experiences, was published in 1926. Virgin Soil Upturned, which earned the Lenin Prize, took 28 years to complete.

The short story The Fate of a Man (1957) was made into a popular Russian film. His collected works were published in eight volumes between 1956 and 1960.

Selected works: Slovo O Rodine (1951); Sudba Cheloveku (1956-57); Early Stories (1966); and Sobranie Sochinenii

Collected Works, 8 volumes, 1956-1958).

1966

Nelly Leonie Sachs

(December 10, 1891-May 12, 1970)

B. Schöneberg, Berlin, Germany

D. Stockholm, Sweden

German poet and dramatist whose Nazi experience turned her into a poignant spokesperson for the grief and yearning of her fellow Jews.

"for her outstanding lyrical and dramatic writing, which interprets Israel's destiny with touching strength"

She shared the Nobel Prize in literature with Shmuel Agnon. She was educated at home due to her frail health. She showed early signs of talent as a dancer, but her protective parents did not encourage her to pursue a profession. She grew up as a very sheltered, introverted young woman and never married. She began writing verse at the age of 17. Romantic and controversial her poems of the 1920s appeared in newspapers. In 1940, after learning that she was destined for a forced-labor camp, she escaped to Sweden. Her best play is Eli: Ein Misterienspiel wom Leiden Israels (A mystery Play of the Sufferings of Israel, 1951). Before she won the Nobel prize on her 75th birthday, she received the 1965 Peace Prize of German publishers. In accepting the award from the land she had fled, she said, "In spite all the horrors of the past I believe in you." She cared for her mother for many years, and supported their existence by translations between Swedish and German. She suffered several breakdowns and spent a number of years in a mental institute. Her poetry is intensely lyrical and shows some influence by German Romanticism. Her first collection of poems appeared in East Berlin under the title In den Wohnungen des Todes (In the Habitations of Death (1947). In 1961 she became the inaugural winner of Nelly Sachs Prize, a literary prize awarded biennially.

Other works: O the Chimneys (1967); and The Seeker and Other Poems (1971).

1966

Shmuel Josef (Joseph) Agnon

(July 17, 1888-February 1970)

B. Buczacz, Eastern Galicia (now Ukraine)

D. Jerusalem, Israel

Hebrew novelist and short-story writer. In Hebrew he is known by the acronym Shai Agnon. He was the first Hebrew writer to win the Nobel Prize. He won the prize jointly with author Nelly Sachs.

"for his profoundly characteristic narrative art with motifs from the life of the Jewish people"

He did not attend school and was schooled by his parents. At the age of 8 he began to write in Hebrew and Yiddish.

His works deal with the conflict between the traditional Jewish life and language and the modern world. They also attempt to recapture the fading traditions of the European shtetl (villages). In wider contest, he also contributed to the broadening the characteristic conception of the narrator's role in literature. He wrote novels and short stories about Jewish life in Europe and Israel. His fiction has profound mystical and psychological overtones, combined social satire with religious themes. Agnon used language and story telling techniques drawn from religious texts and folk literature. He first went to Palestine in 1907 and later changed his name to Agnon, which he took from the title of his first published story Agunot (Forsaken Wives, 1909). In 1910 "Forsaken Wives" was translated into German. In 1912 he published a novella , "Vehaya Ha'akov Lemishor and the Crooked Shall Be Made Straight." He won the Bialik Prize twice (1934 and 1950) and Israel Prize twice (1954 and 1958). He writes about Jewish life, but with his own unique perspective and special touch.

Selected works: Oreah Natah Lalun, 1938 (A Guest for the Night); and Temol Shilshom (Only Yesterday, 1954). His Complete works appeared between 1953 and 1962.

1967

Miguel Ángel Asturias Rosales

(October 19, 1899-June 9, 1974)

B. Guatemala City, Guatemala

D. Madrid, Spain

Guatemalan poet, novelist, and diplomat.

"for his vivid literary achievement, deep-rooted in the national traits and traditions of Indian peoples of Latin America"

He first attended Colegio del Pardo and then Colegio del Parde Solis. He spent a year studying medicine before switching to the faculty of law at the Unversidad de San Carlos de Guatemala in Guatemala City and obtained his law degree in 1923. He participated in the uprising against dictator Manuel Estrada Cabrera. He helped establish Latin-American's contribution to Mainstream Western Culture, and at the same time drew attention to the indigenous cultures, specially those of his native Guatemala. He spent significant time abroad, first in Paris in the 1920s, where he studied anthropology and Italian mythology. Many scholars view him as the first Latin-American novelist to show how the study of anthropology and linguistics could affect the writing of literature. He received many honors and literary awards over the course of his career. While in Paris he also associated with the Surrealist movement and introduced many features of modernist style into Latin-American letters. One of his most famous novels El Señor Presidente, describes life under a ruthless dictator. His very public opposition to dictatorial rule led him spend much of his later time in exile, both in South America and in Europe. In 1966 he won the Soviet Union's Lenin Peace Prize.

Works: Homres de Maiz (Men of Maiz, 1949); El Papa Verde (The Green Pope, 1954); Mulata del tal (The Mulatta and Mr. Fly, 1963); and Viento fuerto, 1950 (Strong Wind/translated by Gregory Rabassa, 1968).

1968

Yasunari Kawabata

(June 14, 1899-April 16, 1972)

B. Osaka, Japan

D. Camakura Kanagawa, Japan

Japanese short-story-writer and novelist.

"for his narrative mastery, which with great sensibility expresses the essence of Japanese mind"

His spare, lyric, subtly-shaped prose won the Nobel Prize for literature, the first Japanese to receive the award. His works have enjoyed broad international appeal and are still widely read. By the time he graduated from Tokyo Imperial University in 1924, he had published several critically acclaimed short stories. By that time he had already caught the attention of Kikuchi Kan and other noted writers and editors through his submissions to Kikuchi's literary magazine the Bungei Shanju. He apparently committed suicide by gassing himself, but a number of close associates, including his widow, consider his death to have been accidental. In 1960 he visited the United States and conducted seminars on Japanese literature at several American universities. His novels are considered typically Japanese in their precise balancing of surface detail and Symbolic meaning. His major themes are loveliness, guilt, and inability to love. In October 1924 Kawabata, katoka Teppei, Yokomitsu Riichi, and a number of young writers started a new literary journal Bungei Jidai (The Artistic Age). He started to achieve recognition with a number of short stories shortly after he graduated, receiving acclaim for the Dancing Girl of Lzu in 1926. As a president of Japanese P.E.N. for many years after the war (1948-95), Kawabata was a driving force behind the translations of Japanese literature into English and other Western languages.

Selected works: Yama no Oto (The sound of the Mountain 1970); and Nemure ru (Sleeping Beauties, 1961).

1969

Samuel Barclay Beckett

(April 13, 1906-December 29, 1989)

B. Foxrock, Dublin, Ireland

D. Paris, France

He was an Irish Avant-grade novelist, playwright, theatre director, and poet who lived in Paris most of his adult life and wrote both in English and French.

"for his writing, which—in new forms for the novel and drama—in the destitution of modern man acquires its elevation"

He is considered by many—one of the last modernists; as an inspiration to many later writers. After graduation with a degree in Romance languages from Trinity College, Dublin, Beckett spent two years in Paris (1928-30) as an exchange lecturer. He is best known for the absurdist drama Waiting for Godot (1952). First performed in Paris on January 5, 1953, the play received worldwide acclaim—the first in a series of critical successes. Shortly after he moved to Paris, a mutual friend introduced him to James Joyce, and quickly he became an apostle of the older writer. He was elected Saoi of Asodána in 1948. At the age of five, Beckett attended a local playschool, where he started to learn music, and then moved to Earlsford House School in the city center near Harcourt Street and in 1919 went to Portora Royal School in Enniskillen. A natural athlete, Beckett excelled at cricket as a left-handed batsman. He studied French, Italian, and English at Trinity College, Dublin from 1923 to 1927. His 16-volume Collected works was published in 1970. Beckett spent some time in London, where in 1931 he published Proust, his critical study of French author Marcel Proust.

Selected works: Molly (1955); Malone Dies (1951); The Unnamable (1953); Murphy (1938); Watt (1953); Texts for Nothing (1955); His plays: Endgame (1957), Happy Days (1961), That Time (1976), and Footfalls (1976).

1970

Alexandr Isayevich Solzhenitsyn

(December 11, 1918-August 3, 2008)

B. Kislovodsk, USSR

D. Moscow, Russia

Russian novelist, dramatist, and historian.

"for the ethical force with which he has pursued the indispensable traditions of Russian literature"

Through his writings, he made the world aware of Gulay, the Soviet's labor camps system, and for these efforts he was exiled from the Soviet Union in 1974. He studied mathematics at Rostov State University at the same time taking correspondence courses from the Moscow Institute of philosophy, literature, and history and graduated at the beginning of World War II. His novels are autobiographical, presenting a vivid account of a man maintaining his freedom against vicious totalitarian repression. Clearly a writer in the 19th century tradition, he is often considered Russia's greatest 20th century novelist. His difficulties with the authorities began on February 8, 1945 when he was arrested for having written critical remarks about Stalin in a letter to a friend intercepted by the censors. Sentenced without a trial for eight years of hard labor, he remained until 1953 in a number of labor camps and brought to America in 1980. A series of writings published late in his life, including the early uncompleted novel Love the Revolution!, chronicle his World War II experience and his growing doubts about the foundations of the Soviet regime. Finally when he was 42 years old, he approached Alexander Tvardovsky, a poet and chief editor of the Novy Mir magazine, with the manuscript of One Day in the Life of Ivan Denisovich. It was published in the edited form in 1962, with the explicit approval from Nikita Khrushchev. The book became an instant hit and sold-out everywhere.

Selected works: The First Circle (1968); The Oak and the Calf (1975); and Three Plays (1981).

1971

Pablo Neruda

(Neftali Ricardo Reyes Basoalto)

(July 12, 1904-September 23, 1973)

B. Parral, Chile

D. Santiago, Chile

Chilean writer and politician.

"for a poetry that with the action of an elemental force brings alive a continent's destiny and dreams"

With his work translated into many languages, he is considered one of the greatest and most influential poets of the 20th century. In 1921 he went to Santiago to study French at the Pedagogical Institute of the University of Chile. He won the first prize in a literature contest in 1921, and three years later he published Twenty Love Poems and A Song of Despair (1924). Following a longstanding Latin-American tradition, the promising young poet was rewarded with consular positions, first in Southern Asia (1927-32) and later in Latin America and Europe. While in Asia, he wrote his powerful if enigmatic Residence on Earth (1933), in which, under the influence of surrealism, he sang of anguish, and solitude in an intensely personal style. During the Spanish Civil War he sided with the Republican cause to which he devoted considerable effort. His social beliefs are reflected in Tercera residencia (Third Residence, 1947), and Canto general (General Song, 1950). His political involvement led him to a seat in the Chilean Senate (1945-48). He told the story of his life in a five volumes of verse (Memorial de Isla Negra, 1964) and in a volume of prose, published posthumously, Confieso que he vivedo (I Confess that I Have Lived, 1974). When Neruda returned to Chile after his Nobel Prize acceptance speech, Salvador Allende invited him to read the Estadio Nacional before 70000 people.

Books of English translations of Neruda are: The Hands of the Day (2008); and The Yellow Heart (1990-2002).

1972

Heinrich Theodor Böll

(December 21, 1917-July 16, 1985)

B. Bologne, German Empire

D. Bonn, Germany

One of Germany's foremost post World War II writers.

"for his writing which through its combination of a broad perspective on his time and a sensitive skill in characterization has contributed to a renewal of German literature"

He was awarded the Georg Büchner award in 1967. He was born to Catholic, pacifist family that, later, opposed to the rise of Nazism. He successfully resisted joining the Hitler Youth during 1930s. He studied German at the University of Cologne. Conscripted into the Wehrmacht, he served in France, Romania, Hungary, and the United States for 6 years, and was wounded four times before he was captured by Americans in April 1945 and was sent to a prison-of-war camp. His early realistic works deal variously with the war and the immediate postwar years. He became a full-time writer at the age of 30. He portrayed Germany after World War II with a deep vision and attacked the materialistic values of the post-war society. He was among the few West Germany writers whose works became popular in both Western and Communist countries. He alienated himself from many sectors of German society by arguing for the just treatment of the German terrorists of the 1970s. In 1954 he received the prize of the Tribune de Paris and in 1960 he became a member of Bavarian Academy of Arts, and many other prizes and awards.

Selected works: Der zug war pünktlich, 1949 (The Train Was on Time); Wo wart du, Adam, 1951 (Where are you, Adam? Billard um halb zehn, 1959 (Billiards at Half-past Nine); Die Spur losen, 1957 (Missing Persons); Das Brot der frühen yahre, 1955 (The Bread of Those Early Years); and Ende einer Dienstfahrt, 1966 (End of a Mission).

1973

Patrick Victor Martindale White

(May 28, 1912-September 30, 1990)

B. Knightsbridge, London, England

D. Sydney, Australia

Australian author who was widely regarded as a major English language novelist of the 20th century.

"for an epic and psychological narrative art which has introduced a new continent into literature"

His fiction freely employs shifting narrative vantage points and streams of consciousness techniques. From 1935 until his death, he published 12 novels, 3 short-story collections and 8 plays. He attended Cheltenham College, England, and Cambridge University (1932) where he studied modern languages. His novels, poems, plays, characterized by a brilliant, incisive style, explore the individual's painful quest for truth, love, and reality. His writings concerned with the dispossessed and lonely, point to the richness complexity of ordinary lives and attempt to show how some people became imbued with spiritual truth. During World War II he served as an intelligence officer with the Royal Air Force in the Middle East and Greece. When the war ended he made several visits to Australia before finally settling on a small farm at Castle Hill, New South Wales. He has tried a number of literary forms.

His first work was a small collection of poems, The Ploughman and Other Poems (1935). A book of short stories, The Burnt Ones, was published in 1964. More important are his Four Plays, published together in 1965: The Ham Funeral, The Season at Sarsaparilla, A Cheery Soul, and Night on Bald Mountain (1961-64). His Reputation, however, rests primarily on his novels: Happy Valley (1939); The Living and the Dead (1941); The Aunt's Story (1948); The Tree of Man (1955); Voss (1957); Riders in the Chariot (1961); The Solid Mandala (1966); The Vivisector (1970); and The Eye of the Storm (1974).

1974

Harry Edmund Martinson

(May 6, 1904-February 11, 1978)

B. Jämshög, Sweden

D. Stockholm, Sweden

Swedish author and poet.

"for writings that catch the dewdrop and reflect the cosmos"

Swedish author and poet. He was elected to the Swedish Academy in 1949. He was awarded joint Nobel Prize in Literature with Eyvind Johnson. He was left orphan at an early age, and after a checkered childhood, in which the children's homes were as numerous as escapees, he went to sea at the age of 16, spent 6 years of his life on board various ships and as a workman in foreign countries. It was for these travels and years of work in environments of all kinds that he later drew material and inspiration for his literary efforts. In 1929 he debuted as a poet. Together with Artur Lunkvist, Gustav Sandgren, Erik Asklund and Joseph Kjllgren, he authored the anthology Fem unga (5 Youths), which introduced Swedish Modernism. His poetry combined an acute eye for and love of nature with a deeply felt humanism. His popular success as a novelist came with the semi-autobiographical Nässlorna (Flowering Nettle), in 1935, about hardships encountered by a young boy in the countryside. It has since been translated into more than 30 languages. One of his most famous work is the poetic cycle Aniara, which is a story of the space craft Aniara, that during a journey through space loses its course, and subsequently aimlessly floats through space, without destination. It was published in 1956, and became an opera in 1959. He committed suicide with a pair of scissors in Karolinska Hospital in Stockholm. His 100th anniversary was celebrated around Sweden in 2004.

Works: Nomad (1931); Vägen ut (The Way Out, 1936); and Den förlorade jaguaren (The Lost Jaguar, 1941).

Sam Majdi

1974

Eyvind Johnson

(July 29, 1900-August 25, 1976)

B. Boden, Norrbotten, Sweden

D. Stockholm, Sweden

Swedish author.

"for a narrative art, farseeing in lands and ages, in the service of freedom"

He became a member of Swedish Academy in 1957, and shared the Nobel Prize with Harry Martinson. His father fell ill about 1904 and he was taken care by his childless aunt and her husband. He did different kind of work, first at the timber sorting town near Sävast, then at the Björn brickworks. Between 1915 and 1919 he was a sawmill worker, a ticket seller and usher at the cinema; then assistant to plumbers and electricians. In the autumn of 1921 he went to Germany by cargo boat to Kiel, by train to Berlin, a few months later to Paris, where he earned his living writing for Swedish papers, as a cement worker, and then as a dishwasher, at a big hotel near the Gare du Nord.

His early life in northern Sweden provided the material for a renewed series of novels, all published before World War II. His most noted works include Här har du ditt liv! (Here is Your Life, 1935), Strändernas Svall (Return to Ithaca, 1946), and Has Nådws Tid (The Days of his Grace, 1690). His first book, De fyra främlingarna (The Four Strangers), a collection of short stories, was finished in the spring of 1924 and published during the autumn. During a winter visit to the North, he finished his second book, which was published in the autumn of 1925. By then he was back in France, where he was to live for over five years.

Selected works: Stad i mörker (Town in Darkness, 1927); Minnas (Remembering, 1928); Natten är här (Night is Here, 1932); Regn i groyningen (Rain at the Dawn, 1933); and Lägg solen (Put Away the Sun, 1951).

1975

Eugenio Montale

(October 12, 1896-September 12, 1981)

B. Genoa, Italy

D. Milan, Italy

Italian poet, prose writer, educator, and translator.

"for his distinctive poetry which, with great artistic sensitivity, has interpreted human values under the sign of an outlook on life with no illusions"

He is one of the few obvious 'true masters' of the last 50 years of Italian literature. He is widely considered the greatest Italian lyric poet since Giacomo Leopardi. In 1961 he was awarded an honorary degree at the University of Rome, also at the University of Milan, Cambridge, and Basel. He contributed genuinely new voice to Italian poetry with his first volume of verse, Ossi di seppia (Cuttlefish Bones, 1925). In 1915 Montale worked as an accountant, but he was left free to follow his passion, frequenting the city's libraries and attending his sister's private philosophy lessons. He also studied opera singing with baritone Ernesto Sivori. He was a self-taught man. During World War1, as a member of the Military Academy of Parma, Montale asked to be sent to the front. He wrote a relatively small number of work. Alongside his imaginative work he was a constant contributor to Italy's most important newspapers, the Corriere della Sera. In 1929 he was asked to be the chairman of the Gabinetto Vissieux Library, a post from which he was expelled in 1938. An uncompromising opponent of fascism under Mussolini, Montale's writings was not invariably dispassionate. Later collections, many of which have been translated in whole or in part, include Le occasion (Occasions, 1939); La bufera e altro (The Storm and Other Poems, 1956); a collection of short stories and prose poems, The Butterfly of Dinard (1956); and Satura (1962-70).

1976

Saul Bellow (Born: Solomon Bellow)

(June 10, 1915-April 5, 2005)

B. Lachine, Quebec, Canada

D. Brookline, Massachusetts, America

Acclaimed American writer, born in Canada of Russian Jewish origin. He also won National medal of Arts in 1988.

"for the human understanding and subtle analysis of contemporary culture that are combined in his work"

He also received the National Book Award three times—for the Adventures of Augie March in 1953, Herzog in 1965, and Mr. Sammler's Planet in 1970. His parents moved from Canada to Chicago when he was 9 years old.

He won a scholarship to the University of Chicago but transferred to Northwestern University, from which he graduated in 1937. Since 1962 he has been a professor at the University and a fellow chairman (1970-76) of its Committee on Social Thought. His first published story, "Two Morning Monologues", appeared in 1941 in the Partisan Review. He won his large popular audience with The Adventures of Augie March. He has often spoken out against the purely formal experimentation of much modern fiction. Bellow received the Peggy V. Helmerich Distinguished Author Award. It is presented annually by the Tulsa Library Trust. In the words of Swedish Nobel Prize Committee, his writing exhibited "exuberant ideas", flashing irony, hilarious comedy and burning compassion the mixture of rich picaresque novel and subtle analysis of our culture, of penetrating adventure, drastic and tragic episodes in quick succession interspersed with philosophic conversation.

Selected works and prizes: Humboldt's Gift (1975); Pulitzer Prize (1976); The Dean's December (1928); More Die of Heartbreak (1987); Mosby's Memoirs (1968); and To Jerusalem and Back (1976).

1977

Vicente Pio Marcelino Cirilo

Aleixandre Y Merlo

(April 26, 1898-December 13, 1984)

B. Seville, Spain

D. Madrid, Spain

Spanish poet, was part of Generation of '27.

"for a creative poetic writing which illuminates man's condition in the cosmos and in present day society, at the same time representing the great renewal of traditions of Spanish poetry between the wars"

His early poems, which he wrote mostly in free verse, is highly surrealistic. He spent his early childhood in Málaga and moved to Madrid in 1909. He studied law at the University of Madrid. He first suffered kidney tuberculosis in 1925, which left him invalid throughout his life. Sickness left its mark on his poetry—desperate song of his journey from annihilation, evasion, and darkness to an affirmation of life, love, and light. A member of a group called the Generation of 1927, he won the National Literature Prize for his work Destruction, or Love in 1933. In 1944, he published The Shadow of Paradise, the poetry where he first began to concentrate on themes such as fellowship, friendliness, and spiritual unity. His later books of poetry include History of the Heart (1954) and In a Vast Dominion (1962). In 1950, he became a member of Spanish Academy. His books and anthologies have been published up to the present day. In later collections he portrays man as a being who suffers and dies within a temporal framework but nevertheless remains part of a vast cosmic reality. In early collections of poetry include the Passion of the Earth (1935) and Destruction or Love. Selections of his work were translated into English in Twenty Poems of Vicente Aleixandre (1977), and a Longing for the Light.

1978

Isaac Bashevis Singer (Izac Zinger)

(November 21, 1904-July 24, 1991)

B. Leoncin, Congress, Poland

D. Surfside, Florida, U.S.A.

Polish-born American author and one of the leading figures in the Yiddish literary movement.

"for his impassioned narrative art which, with roots in a Polish-Jewish cultural tradition, brings universal human conditions to life"

Emerson street in Surfside, Florida is named Isaac Bashevis Boulevard in his honor. He won two U.S. National Book Awards, one in Children's Literature for his memoir A Day of Pleasure. In brilliantly crafted novels, short stories, and plays he evoked the manners, morals, and mystical learnings of the pre-World War II Jewish communities of Eastern Europe. Before the German invasion and the Holocaust, Singer emigrated from Poland to the United States due to the growing Nazi threat in neighboring Germany. Gimpel the Fool (1957) and the Spinoza of Market Street (1961) are among the best-loved stories. Scum (1991) published in the year after his death, depicts Warsaw at the turn of the century. His famous trilogy, The Family Moskat (1950), The Manor (1967), and The Estate (1970), is a family epic that traces the history of the Jews in Poland from the anti-tsarist uprisings of 1863 to World War II. A born story teller, he was usually at his best in his short stories, which have been republished in his Collected Short Stories (1982). He wrote many of his books for children. His autobiographical works have been published under the title Love and Exile (1984). His novel Enemies: A Love Story (1972) appeared as a film in 1989.

Selected Works: Magicians of Lubin (1960); The Spinoza of Market Street (1963); The Slave (1962); The Wicked City (1972); The King of the Fields (1988); Reaches of Heaven (1980); and Shadow on the Hudson (1997).

1979

Odysseus Elytis

(November 2, 1911-March 18, 1996)

B. Heraklion, Crete, Germany

D. Athens, Greece

Greek poet regarded as a major exponent of romantic modernism in Greece and the world.

"for his poetry, which, against the background of Greek tradition, depicts with sensuous strength and intellectual clear-sightedness modern man's struggle for freedom and creativeness"

He had been twice Program Director of the Greek National Education (1945-46 and 1953-54). He attended courses as an editor at the Law School at University of Athens. He came to prominence with poems characterized by their bright Aegean setting, their affirmation of life and joy, and their debt to surrealism. World War II gave his outlook an added depth, which is apparent in his later collections. His masterpiece, Seemly It Is (1959) is a vast and complex spiritual autobiography that makes full use of the resources of the Greek language and Greek history. In 1935 he published his first poem in the journal New Letters. His entry with a distinctively earthy and original form assisted to inaugurate a new era in Greek poetry and its subsequent reform after the World War II. His poetry has marked, through an active presence of over forty years, a broad spectrum of subject matter and realistic touch with an emphasis on the expression of that which is rarefied and passionate. From 1967-72, under the German military junta of 1967-74, Elytis exiled himself to Paris. He was a member of the Association of German-Art Critics, AICA-Hellas, International Association of Art Critics.

Works: Orientations (1939); The Sovereign Sun (1971); The Trills of Love (1973); The Monogram (1972); Maria Nefeli (1978); Private Way (1990); and In White (1992).

1980

Czeslaw Milosz

(June 30, 1911-August 14, 2004)

B. Šeteiniai, near Kedainia, Lithuania

D. Kraków, Poland

Polish-American poet, essayist, and critic.

"who, with uncompromising clear-sightedness voices man's exposed condition in a world of conflicts"

His first volume of poetry was published in 1934, after receiving his law degree that year. In 1960 he emigrated to the U.S., and in 1970 he became a U.S. citizen. Although he is ranked as the greatest contemporary Polish poet, he is best known outside Poland as the author of such political works as the essay collections Captive Mind (1953), and Native Realm (1959). In 1953 he received Prix Littéraire Européen. In 1960 he was invited by the University of California and moved to Berkeley. He was professor of Slavic Languages and Literature. Active in the Warsaw resistance during World War II, he served as a diplomat in the postwar Polish government. In 1951 he sought political asylum in France, however, and since 1960 he has lived and taught in the U.S. His poems in English translation have been published in Collected Poems (1931-87), Provinces: poems (1987-91), The Year of the Hunter (1994), and Facing the River (1995). He translated the Old Testament Psalms into Polish. In the diplomatic service of the People's Polish since 1915, he broke with the government in 1951 and settled in France where he wrote several books in prose. Presented with an award for poetry translation from the Polish P.E.N. Club in Warsaw in 1974; a Guggenheim Fellow for poetry in 1976; received an honorary degree Doctor of Letters from the University of Michigan Ann Arbor in 1977; received the Berkeley Citation in 1978; and nominated by the Academic Senate for a "Research Lecturer" of 1979-90.

1981

Elias Canetti

(July 5, 1905-August 14, 1994)

B. Ruse, Bulgaria

D. Zürich, Switzerland

Bulgarian-born novelist of Sephardi Jewish Ancestry.

"for writings marked by a broad outlook, a wealth of ideas and artistic power"

He graduated from high school in Frankfurt. He went back to Vienna in 1924 to study chemistry, but his primary interest during the years in Vienna became philosophy and literature. Introduced into the literary circles of first-republic-Vienna, he started writing. He gained a degree in chemistry from the University of Vienna in 1929, but he never worked as a chemist. He wrote in German and his work explores the emotions of the individual at odds, with the society around him. Despite being a German writer, Canetti settled and stayed in England until the 1970s, receiving the British citizenship in 1952. For his last 20 years he mostly lived in Zürich. He is known chiefly for his novel Auto-da-Fé (Die Blendung, 1935), and for Masse und Macht (Crowd and Power, 1960). Elias spent his childhood years, from 1905 to 1911, in Ruse until the family moved to England. In 1912 his father died suddenly, and his mother moved with their children to Vienna in the same year. They lived in Vienna from the time Canetti was aged seven onwards. His mother insisted that he speak German, and taught it to him. By this time Canetti already spoke Latino (his mother tongue), Bulgarian, English and some French (he studied the latter two in the one year in England).

Canetti published three volumes of autobiography: Die gerettete Zunge (The Tongue Set Free, 1977); Die Fackel im Ohr (The Torch in My Ear, 1980); and Das Augenspiel (The Play of the Eyes, 1985).

1982

Gabriel José de la Concordia García Márquez

(March 6, 1927-April 17, 2014)

B. Aracataca, Magdelena, Colombia

D. Mexico City, Mexico

Colombian novelist, short-story writer, screen writer and journalist. The uncertain old man whose real existence was the simplest of his enigmas.

"for his novels and short-stories, in which the fantastic and the realistic are combined in a richly composed world of imagination, reflecting a continent's life and conflicts"

Affectionately known as "Gabo" throughout Latin America, he is considered one of the most significant authors of the 20th century. He pursued a self-directed education that resulted in his leaving law school in a career in journalism. From early on, he showed no inhibitions in his criticism of Colombian and foreign politics. He started as a journalist, and has written many acclaimed non-fictions and short-stories, but is best-known for his novels, such as One Hundred Years of Solitude (1967) and Love in the Time of Cholera (1985). His works have achieved significant critical acclaim and widespread commercial success which uses magical elements and events in otherwise ordinary and realistic situations. Some of his works are set in a fictional village called Mocondo, and most of them express the theme of solitude. In 1954 he was sent to Rome on an assignment for his newspaper, and since then he has mostly lived abroad—in Paris, New York, Barcelona and Mexico, in a more or less—compulsory exile. On his death, Juan Manual Santos, the President of Colombia, described him as "the greatest Colombian ever lived".

Some of his works: In Evil Hour (1962); The Autumn of Patriarch (1975); Friendship is Beautiful (2009); Chronicle of a Death Foretold (1981); and The Abduction 1983).

1983

Sir William Gerald Golding

(September 19, 1911- June 10, 1993)

B. St. Columb Minor, Cornwall, England

D. Perranarworthal, Cornwall, England

English novelist, essayist and poet.

"for his novels which, with perspicuity of realistic narrative art and the diversity and universality of myth, illuminate the human condition in the world of today"

He was best known for his novel Lord of the Flies. He was also awarded the Booker Prize in literature for his novel Rites of Passage in 1980. He studied English literature and philosophy at Oxford and served in the Royal Navy during World War II. His First novel Lord of the Flies, 1954 (film, 1963), introduced on of the recurrent theme of his fiction—the conflict between humanity's innate barbarism and the civilizing influence of reason.

In addition to his novels, he published a play, The Brass Butterfly (1958); a book of verse, Poems (1934); and the essay collections The Hot Gates (1965) and A Moving Target (1982). He was knighted in 1988. His first novel was critically acclaimed and commercially successful and became required reading in English courses in England and in the U.S. It tells of a group of boys, stranded on the island after a plane crash, who deteriorate in savagery in spite of the efforts of few of them to organize a civilized community. The Inheritors (1955) reaches into prehistory, advancing the thesis that humankind's evolutionary ancestors, "the fire-builders" triumphed over a gentler race as much by violence and deceit as by natural superiority.

Other works: Pincher Martin (1956); Free Fall (1959); The Spire (1964); Darkness Visible (1979); The historical trilogy Rites of Passage (1981); Close Quarters (1987); Fire Down Below (1989); The Pyramid (1967); The Hot Gates (1965); and The Paper Men (1984).

1984

Jaroslav Seifert

(September 23, 1901-January 10, 1986)

B. Žižkov, suburb of Prague, Austria-Hungary

D. Prague, Czechoslovakia

Czech writer, poet, and journalist. He was the first Czech to win the Nobel prize for literature. He belonged to the extreme left wing of the Social Democratic Party. In 1920s he was considered a leading representative of the Czechoslovakian artistic Avant-grade.

"for his poetry which endowed with freshness, sensuality and rich inventiveness provides a liberating image of the indomitable spirit and versatility of man"

He was the member of the Communist Party, the editor of a number of Communist newspapers and magazines—Rovnost, Srsatec, and Reflektor—and the employee of a communist publishing house. He was one of the founders of the journal Devětsil. In 1949 he left journalism and began to devote himself exclusively to literature. He made his debut in 1918 and published his first collection of poems in 1921. During the years 1945-48, he edited the literary monthly Kytice. His poetry was awarded important state prizes in 1936, 1955, and 1968. In 1967 he was designated National Artist. He was the official Chairman of Czechoslovak Writer's Union (1968-70). Due to bad health he was not present at the award ceremony, and so his daughter received it in his name. Even though it was a matter of great importance, there was only a brief remark of the award in the state-controlled media. In 1977 he was on the signatories of Chapter 77 to the repressive regime of the time. During the German occupation, he was the editor of the daily Národni práce and monthly Kytice.

Some of his works: Somá Láska (1923); Hvězdy nad rajskou zahradou (1929); Jablko z Klina (1933); Jaro Sbohen (1937); Ruka a Plamen (1948); Zrnka révy (1965); and Halleyova Kometa (1967).

1985

Claude Eugène Henri Simon

(October 10, 1913-July 6, 2005)

B. Tananarive, Madagascar

D. Paris, France

French novelist.

"who in his novel combines the poet's and the painter's creativeness with a deepened awareness of time in the depiction of human condition"

He also received the prize of "Express" for La Route Des Flanders (The Flanders Road, 1960) in 1961 and Médicis prize for "Historie" in 1967. The University of East Anglia made him honorary doctor in 1973. He is a writer whose works are among the most authentic representatives of nouveau roman (new novel) that emerged in 1950s. After studies at Paris, Oxford, and Cambridge, he traveled widely and then fought in World War II. He defined his goals: to challenge the fragmentation of his time and to rediscover the permanence of objects and people evidenced by their survival through the upheavals of contemporary history. He treated the turmoil of the Spanish Civil War in La Corde Raide (The Tightrope, 1947). Simon's style is a mixture of narration and stream of consciousness, lacking all punctuation and heavy with 1000 word sentences, Simon attempted to capture the very progression of life. He was captured by Germans in May 1940, escaped and joined the French Resistance, managing to complete his first novella Tricheur (The Trikester, 1945). Many critics consider his novels, especially La Route des Flanders, to be his most important work.

Other works: Le Sacre du Printemps (The Rite of Spring, 1954)). Four novels: L' Herbe (The Grass, 1958), La Palace (The Palace, 1962); Leçon de choses (Lesson in Things, 1975); Le tramway (The Trolley, 2001); and Gulliver (1952).

1986

Wole Soyinka (Akinwande Oluwole)

(July 13, 1934...

B. Abeokuta, Nigeria Protectorate

Nigerian writer, poet, and playwright. Some consider him Africa's most distinguished playwright. He is the first African to receive the Nobel Prize.

"Who in a wide cultural perspective and with poetic overtones fashions the drama of existence"

Primarily a playwright, he has been influential in the development of modern Nigerian drama. After study in Nigeria and the UK, he worked with the Royal Court Theatre in London. His plays, which have received international attention, range from satirical comedy to powerful tragedy. In his writings he often contrasts traditional Nigerian values with values of modern world and finds both adequate. He attended the University of Ibadan in Nigeria and graduated from the University of Leeds in 1958. With the outbreak of civil war in Nigeria in 1967, he was arrested for treason. After his release from prison in 1969 he lived for periods of time in exile and taught at universities in Africa, Europe, and the U.S. He has been an implacable, consistent and outspoken critic of many Nigerian dictators, and political tyrannies worldwide including the Mugabe regime. In 1994, he was designated United Nations Educational, Scientific and Cultural (UNESCO) Goodwill Ambassador for the promotion of African culture, human rights, freedom of expression, media and communication.

His works: Plays—The Lion and the Jewel (1959); A Dance of the Forests (1960); The Trials of Brother Jero (1961); The Strong Breed (1962); The Road (1964); A Play of Giants (1984). Poems—Indandre and Other Poems (1967); The Interpreters (1965) is a novel; and A Man Died: Prison Notes of Wole Soyinka (1972).

1987

Joseph Aleksandrovich Brodsky

(May 24, 1940-Jan 28, 1996)

B. Leningrad, Russia

D. New York City, New York, America

Soviet-Russian-American poet and essayist.

He was appointed Poet Laureate Consultant to the Library of Congress in 1991 and received Struga Poetry Evenings Golden Wreath.

"for an all-embracing authorship, imbued with clarity of thought and poetic intensity"

In early childhood he survived the Siege of Leningrad. When he was 15, Brodsky left school and tried to enter the School Submariners without success. He went to work as a milling machine operator. Later, having decided to become a physician, he worked at a morgue at the Kresty prison. He subsequently held a variety of jobs at a hospital, in a ship's boiler room, and on geological expeditions. At the same time, Brodsky engaged in a program of self-education. He learned English and Polish and acquired a deep interest in classical philosophy, religion, mythology, and English and American poetry. He began writing his own poetry and producing literary translations around 1957. The young Brodsky was encouraged and influenced by the poet Anna Akhmatova who called some of his verses 'enchanting". In 1963, he was arrested and in 1964 charged with parasitism by the soviet authorities. In 1986, Farrar, Straus, and Girous published a collection of his essays on the arts and politics, which won the National Book Critic's Award for criticism and also a collection of his poetry, To Urania, and in 1992 a collection of essays about Venice, Watermark. Throughout his career he wrote in Russian and English, self translating and working with poet-translators.

Other works: A Part of Speech (1977); Discovery (1999); and Less Than One, Selected Essays (1986).

1988

Naguib Mahfouz

(December 11, 1911-August 30, 2006)

B. Cairo, Egypt

D. Cairo, Egypt

Egyptian novelist. He is regarded as one of the first contemporary writers of Arabic literature, along with Tawfiq-al-Hakim, to explore themes of existentialism.

"who, through works rich in nuance-now clear-sightedly realistic, now evocatively ambiguous—has formed an Arabian narrative art that applies to all mankind"

He published over 50 novels, over 350 short stories, dozens of movie scripts and 5 plays over a 70-year career. Many of his works have been made into Arabic and foreign-language films. In his childhood he read extensively. His family were devout Muslims and had a strictly Islamic upbringing. The Egyptian Revolution of 1919 had strong effect on Mahfouz. He entered the King Fuad University, now known as the University of Cairo, where he studied philosophy, graduating in 1934. Then he decided to become a professional writer. He worked as a journalist at er-Risala, and contributed to Al-Hilal and Al-Ahram. A long civil servant, Mahfouz served in the Ministry of Mortmain Endowments, then as director of Censorship in the Bureau of Art, director of the Foundation for the support of the Cinema, and finally the Ministry of Culture.

In his old age he became nearly blind, though he continued to write, he had difficulties in holding a pen or a pencil. Prior to his death, he suffered from a bleeding ulcer, kidney problems, and cardiac failure.

Some of his works: Abath Al-Aqdar (Mockery of the Fates, 1939); Radubis (1943); Kifah Tibah (The Struggle of Tyba, 1944); Cairo Trilogy (Palace Walk, Palace of Desire, and Sugar Street), an immense monumental work of 1500 pages; Chitchat on the Nile (1966); and The Children of Gebelawi (Children of our Alley, 1959).

1989

Camilo José Cela Y Trulock

(May 11, 1916-January 17, 2002)

B. Padrón, Galicia, Spain

D. Madrid, Spain

An influential Spanish novelist and short story writer associated with the Generation of 1936 movement.

"for a rich and intensive prose, which with restrained compassion forms a challenging vision of man's vulnerability"

Before he became a professional writer, Cela attended the University of Madrid, where he briefly pursued a law degree. He also fought in Spanish War on the side of Franco. After the war, Cela dedicated himself to newspaper work. He published his first novel, La Familia de Pascual Duarte (The Family of Pascual Duarte). This novel is of particular importance as it played a large part in shaping the direction of the post-war Spanish novel.

In 1948 he published two travel books Viaje la Alcarria (Journey to Alcarria) and Del Miño al Bidasoa (From Minho to Bidasoa). His best known work, La Colmena (The Hive) was published in 1951, featuring more than 300 characters and style showing the influence of both realism and contemporary English and French language authors such as Joyce and Sartre. He published two travel books from the late 1960s, with the publishing of San Camilo in 1936, Cela's work became increasingly experimental. In 1957 he was appointed a member of the Real Academia Española. He was also named Marquis of Iria Flavia by King Juan Carlos. In recognition of his contributions in literature, Cela was ennobled on May 17, 1996 by King Juan Carlos, who gave Cela the hereditary title of Marqués de Ira Flavia. He was appointed Royal Senator in the Constituent Cortes, where he exerted some influence in the wording of the Spanish Constitution of 1978.

1990

Octavio Paz Lozano

(March 31, 1914-April 19, 1998)

B. Mexico City, Mexico

D. Mexico City, Mexico

Mexican writer, poet, and diplomat.

He became one of the founders of the journal Taller (Workshop) in 1938.

"for impassioned writing with wide horizons, characterized by sensuous intelligence and humanistic integrity"

Because of his family's public support of Emiliano Zapato they were forced into exile after Zapato's assassination. They served their exile in the United States. He was introduced to literature early in his life through the influence of his grandfather's library. As a teenager in 1931 under the influence of D.H. Lawrence, Paz published his first poems, Like Cabellera. Two years later he published Luna Silvestre (Wild Moon), a collection of poems. In 1932, with some friends, he founded his first literary review, Brandal. In 1937 he was invited to the Second International Writers Congress in Defence of Culture in Spain during the country's Civil War. During the 1920s, he discovered the European poets Gerardo Diego, Juan Ramón Jiménez, and Antonio Machodo, Spanish writers who had a great influence on his early writings. From 1970 to 1974, he lectured at Harvard University, where he held the Charles Eliot Norton Professorship. He studied at Colegio Williams. He won the 1977 Jerusalem Prize on the theme of individual and in 1980 he was awarded an honorary doctorate from Harvard.

Works: In India, Paz completed several works, including El mono gramático (The Monkey Grammarian) and Ladera Este (Eastern Slope).

Awards: Peace Prize of German Book Trade; Miguel de Cervantes Prize (1981); Jerusalem Prize; Alfonso Reyes Prize; and Alexis de Tocqueville Prize.

1991

Nadine Gordimer

(November 20, 1923-July 13, 2014)

B. Springs, South Africa

D. Johannesburg, South Africa

African writer and political activist. Her writings long dealt with moral and racial issues, particularly in South Africa.

"who through her magnificent epic writing has—in the words of Alfred Nobel—been of very great benefit to humanity"

She was active in the anti-apartheid movement, joining the African National Congress during the days when the Organization was banned. She has recently been active in HIV/AIDS causes. Her parents were both Jewish immigrants. She was educated at a Catholic convent school. Homebound and often isolated, she began writing at an early age, and published her first stories in 1937. Her first published work was a short story for children, "The Quest for Seen Gold", which appeared in the Children's Sunday Express in 1937; Come Again Tomorrow, another children's story appeared in Forum around the same time. At the age of 16, she had her first adult fiction published. She studied for a year at the University of Witwatersrand.

She did not complete her degree, but moved to Johannesburg in 1948, where she lived ever since. Her first novel The Lying Days, was published in 1953. When Nelson Mandela was released from prison in 1990, Gordimer was one of the first people he wanted to see. She had begun to achieve international recognition, receiving her first major award in 1961.

Works: The World of Strangers (1958); Occasion for Loving (1963); The Guest of Honor (1970); Burger's Daughter (1979); and No Time Like the Present (2012).

Awards and honors: Grand Aigle d'Or (France, 1975); And Nelly Sachs Prize (Germany, 1986).

1992

Derek Alton Walcott

(Jan 23, 1930…

B. Castries, Saint Lucia, West Indies

Caribbean poet, playwright, writer and visual artist, noted for works that explore the Caribbean cultural experience. He is widely considered the finest modern poet and playwright.

"for a poetic oeuvre of great luminosity, sustained by a historical vision, the outcome of a multicultural commitment"

After completing his education at the University of the West Indies in Jamaica, Walcott taught at several West Indian schools before settling in Jamaica. There, while working as a journalist, he founded the Trinidad Workshop in 1959, produced his plays (and others) since that time, remains active with its Board of Directors. He also founded Boston Playwright's Theatre at Boston University in 1981. He continues to give readings and lectures throughout the world. He studied as a writer, becoming "an elated , exuberant poet madly in love with English" and strongly influenced my modernist poets such as T.S. Eliot and Ezra Pound. Some 20 of his plays have been produced in the West Indies, Europe, and the United States. His many volumes of poetry include In a Green Night (1962), his first successful collection; the Autobiographical Another Life (1973); The Collected Poems (1948-1984); and the epic-length Odyssey"—Inspired Omeros (1990).

Other works: Selected Poems (1964); The Castaway and Other Poems (1965); Midsummer (1984); The Bounty (1997); Tiepolo's Hound (2000); Prodigal (2004).

Selected Poems (2007); and White Egrets (2010).

Plays: Wine of the Country (1953); In a Fine Castle (1970); and Walker and the Ghost Dance (2002).

1993

Toni Morrison (Chloe Ardelia Wofford)

(February 18, 1931…

B. Lorain, Ohio, United States

American author, educator and poet. Her novels are known for epic themes, vivid dialogues, and richly detailed black characters. She also won a Pulitzer Prize for novel Beloved in 1988.

"who in novels characterized by visionary force and poetic import, gives life to an essential aspect of American Reality"

In 1949 she entered Howard University to study English and received a B.A. in English, then earned a Master of Arts Degree, from Cornell University in 1955, for which she wrote a thesis on suicide in the works of William Faulkner and Virginia Woolf. After graduating, Morrison became an English instructor at Texas Southern University in Houston, Texas (1955-57). As an editor Morrison played an important role in bringing black literature into the mainstream. Song of Solomon brought her national attention. In 1987 her novel Beloved became a critical success. In 1984 she was appointed an Albert Schweitzer Chair at Albany, The State University of New York. From her first novels, The Bluest Eyes (1970) and Sula (1973), Morrison has portrayed to great effect the double-edged character of black lives—shaped, enriched, and threatened from inside their own histories and culture, stifled and oppressed by the white world outside. Song of Solomon (1977) won the National Book Critic Award.

From 1889 until her retirement in 2006, Morrison held the Robert F. Cohen Chair in the Humanities at Princeton University.

Other works: Tar Baby (1981); Jazz (1992); Paradise (1999); Love (2003); and A Mercy (2008).

Children's literature (with Slade Morrison): The Big Box (1999); and The Book of Mean People (2002).

1994

Kenzaburō Ōe

(January 31, 1935....

B. Uchiko, Ehime, Prefecture, Japan

A major figure in contemporary Japanese literature.

writing period: 1950-present

"who with poetic force creates an imagined world, where life and myth condense to form a disconcerting picture of the human predicament today"

Deeply influenced by American and French literature and literature theory, engage with political, social philosophy issues including nuclear weapons, social nonconformist and existentialism. At the age of 18 he began to study French literature at the University of Tokyo, where he wrote his dissertation on the work of Jean-Paul Sartre. He began publishing stories in 1955 while still a student.

Japan's defeat in the war in 1945 brought enormous change, even to the remote village. Young Ōe took democracy straight to his heart. So strong was his desire for democracy that he decided to leave for Tokyo; leave the village of his forefathers, the life they had lived and preserved, out of sheer belief that the city offered him an opportunity to knock at the door of democracy, the door that would leave him to a future freedom on paths that stretched out to the world. In 1960 he met Mao Zedong on a trip to China. He also went to Russia and Europe the following year, visiting Sartre in Paris.

His works: Bud Nipping, Lamb Shooting (1958); The Youth Who Came Late (1961); A Personal Matter (1964); Hiroshima Notes (1965); The Silent Cry (1967); Teach Us to Outgrow Our Madness (1977); My Deluged Soul (1973); and Rouse Up O Young Men of the New Age (1983).

Honors: Akutagawa Prize (1958); Shinchosha Literary Prize (1983); Noma Prize (1973); and Order of Culture (1994—refused).

1995

Seamus Heaney

(April 13, 1939-August 30, 2013)

B. Near Castledawson, Northern Ireland

D. Dublin, Ireland

Irish poet, writer, and lecturer, he currently lives in

Dublin, Ireland.

"for works of lyrical beauty and ethical depth, which exalt everyday miracles and the living past"

He is ranked by many the finest Irish poet since William Butler Yeats. His work draws its most vital images from the Irish soil and the act of working it, and from the Irish past, specially of Northern Island. From the publication of his first collection, Death of a Naturalist (1966) his work has been enthusiastically received. When he was 12 years old, Seams won a scholarship to St. Columb's College, a Catholic boarding school where he was taught Latin and Irish. In the course of his career, Heaney has always contributed to the promotion of artistic and educational causes, both in Ireland and abroad. He is a member of Aosdána, the Irish academy of artists and writers, and a foreign member of the American Academy of Arts and Letters. In 1953, his family moved to Bellaghy, a few miles away, which is now a family home. In 1957 he traveled to Belfast to study English Language and Latin at the Queen's University of Belfast. He graduated in 1961 with a First Class Honors degree. His first book Eleven Poems, was published in November 1965 for the Queen's University Festival. In 1967, Faber and Faber published his first major volume Death of a Naturalist. Also in 1966, he was appointed a lecturer in Modern English Literature at Queen's University in Belfast.

Other works: Wintering Out (1972); North (1975); Field Work (1979); Seeing Things (1991), and several prose collections.

1996

Wisława Szymborska

(July 2, 1923-February 1st, 2012)

B. Kórnik, in Western Poland

D. Kraków, Poland

Polish poet, essayist, and translator whose intelligent and emphatic explorations of philosophical, moral, ethical issues won her the Nobel Prize in literature.

"for poetry that with ironic precision allows the historical and biological context to come to light in fragments of human reality"

Since 1931 she has been living in Kraków, where during 1945-48 she studied Polish at the Jagiellonian University.

In Poland her books reach sales rivaling prominent prose authors. She frequently employs literary devices such As irony paradox, contradiction and understatement, to illuminate philosophical themes and obsessions. Her reputation rests on relatively small body of work. She is often described to the point of shyness. She has been cherished by Polish contemporaries and her poetry has been set to music by Zbigniew Preisner. Her work has been translated into many European languages, as well as Arabic, Hebrew, Japanese and Chinese. When World War II broke out in 1939 she continued education in underground lessons. In 1945 she took up studies of Polish language and literature before switching to sociology. In 1945, she published her first poem Szukam Slowa (I Seek the Word). Her poems continued to be published in various newspapers and periodicals for a number of years.

Prizes and awards: The City of Kraków Prize for Literature (1934); The Polish Ministry of Culture Prize (1963); The Goethe Prize (1991); Herder Prize (1995); and The Polish PEN Club Prize (1996).

Some of her works: Sól (Salt, 1962); and Sto Pociech (No End of Fun (1967); (Moments, 2002); and Putaj (Here, 2009).

1997

Dario Fo

(March 24, 1926...

B. San Giano, Italy

Italian artist, playwright, theatre director, and composer.

In 2007 he was ranked joint seventh with Stephen Hawking in the Telegraph's list of 100 greatest living geniuses.

"who emulates the jesters of the Middle Ages in scourging authority and upholding the dignity of the downtrodden"

His many plays have been produced successfully in more than 30 countries—although his fame is greatest in Italy, where the objects of his satire often reside. One of his most popular plays is Mistero Buffo (Comic Mystery) (1969), a set of black-humor sketches for a single actor. Accidental Death of an Anarchist (1970); an absurdist satire based on the 1969 murder of an Italian leftist. In 1940 he moved to Milan to study at the Brera Art Academy, but World War II intervened. His family was active in anti-fascist resistance and reputedly he helped his father to smuggle refugees and allied soldiers to Switzerland. In 1951 Fo met Franca Rame. After a slow start, they became engaged and were Married on June 24, 1954. In the same year he was invited to perform a radio play Cocirico in RAI, Italian national radio. In 1955 Fo and Rame worked in movie production in Rome. Fo became a screen writer and worked for many productions. Fo wrote scripts, acted, directed, and designed costumes. In 1961 Fo's plays began to play in Sweden and Poland. In 1981 Cambridge's American Repertory Theatre invited Fo to perform in the Italian Festival in New York.

His works: Archangels Don't Play Pinball (1959); He who Steels a Foot is Lucky in Love (1961); The Pope and the Witch (1989); The Devil with Boobs (1997); Comical mystery (1969); The Pregnant man (1977); and The People's War in Chile (1973).

1998

José de Sousa Saramago

(November 16, 1922- June 18, 2010)

B. Azinhaga, Santarém, Portugal

D. Tias, Lanzarote, Spain

Portuguese novelist, playwright, and journalist

"who with parables sustained by imagination, compassion and irony continually enables us once again to apprehend an elusory reality"

He has combined his work myths, history of his own country, and surrealistic imagination. After trying different jobs in the civil service, he worked for a publishing company for 12 years and then for newspapers. Although he was a good pupil, his parents were unable to keep him in grammar school, and instead moved to a technical school. In 1940, Fo moved to Milan to study at the Brera Academy. After graduating, he worked as a car mechanic for two years. Later he worked as a translator, then as a journalist. He was an assistant editor of the newspaper Diário de Noticias, a position he had to leave after the political events in 1975. In 1947 he published his first book, a novel that he entitled Widows, but which for editorial reasons appeared as The Land of Sin. For 19 years, till 1966, when he published Possible Poems, a poetry book that marked his return to literature, he was absent from Portuguese literature scene. In 1970 he published another book of poems, probably Joy, and in 1971 and 1973 respectively he published From this World and the Other and The Traveler's Baggage. His first novel Manual de Pintura Caligrafia (Manual of Painting and Calligraphy) appeared in 1977. His books have been translated into 25 languages. He founded the National Front for the Defence of Culture (Lisbon, 1922).

Other works: Terra do Pacado (Land of Sin, 1947); Levantado do Chô (Raised From the Ground, 1980); Death of Ricardo Reis (1984); and La Caverna (The Cave, 2000).

1999

Günter Wilhelm Grass

(October 16, 1927...

B. Danzig-Langfuhr, Free City of Danzig (now in Poland).

German author and playwright. In 1945 he reached West Germany as a homeless refugee after the expulsion of Germans from Poland.

"whose frolicsome black fables portray the forgotten face of history"

He is considered one of the foremost literary figures of postwar Germany. His strong commitment to political ideas is manifested in satiric Rabelaisian novels and plays. He came as a refugee to West Germany in 1945. The Tin Drum (1959), is a key text in European magic realism, and the first part of his Danzig Trilogy. He has been an active supporter of the Social Democratic Party of Germany. In 1946 and 47 he worked in a mine and received a stonemason's education. For many years he studied sculpture and graphic at Düsseldorf and Berlin Universities. He also worked as an author and traveled frequently. From 1985 to 1986 he held the presidency of Berlin Academy of Arts. The Tin Drum and The Flounders (1977) are among his most acclaimed works. The Tin Drum was adapted into a film, which won both the 1979 Palme d'Or and the Academy Award for Best Foreign Language Film. Drafted into the Labor Service toward the end of World War II, he was wounded and taken prisoner in 1940. As a committed artist and antifascist, he said that "to be engaged to act." His dramatic works reveal the influence of the theatre of the absurd and the epic theatre of Bertolt Brecht. His political activities and his sense of commitment inform his later works as well.

Other works: Cat and Mouse (1961); Dog Years (1963); a German Tragedy (1965); From the Diary of a Snail (1972); The Meeting at the Telgte (1981); The Rat (1986); Two States—One Nation (1990); and Die Box (2008).

2000

Gao Xingjian

(January 4, 1940 …

B. Ganzhou, Jiangxi, China

French Chinese émigré novelist, dramatist, and critic.

He is also a noted translator, screenwriter, and a celebrated painter. He was granted French citizenship in 1997.

"for an oeuvre of universal validity, bitter insights and linguistic ingenuity, which has opened new paths for the Chinese novel and drama"

In 1992 he was awarded the Chevalier de l'Ordre des Arts et des Lettres by French Government. Under his mother's influence, Gao enjoyed painting, writing and theatre very much when he was a little boy. During his middle school years, he read lots of literature translated from the West, and studied sketch, ink and wash painting and clay sculpture under the guidance of Yun Zongying. In May 1979, he visited Paris with Chinese writers including Ba Jin, and served as a French translator in the group. By 1987, Gao had shifted to Bagnolet, a city adjacent to Paris, France. He graduated in 1957. He entered Beijing Foreign Studies University (BFSU). In 1962 he graduated from the Department of French, and then entered the Chinese International Bookstore, where he became a professional translator. He taught as a Chinese teacher in Gangkou Middle School for a short time. In 1977 he worked for the Committee of Foreign Relationship, Chinese Association of Writers. He is known as a pioneer of absurdist drama in Paris. He was awarded Lions Award by the New York Public Library in 2006.

His works: Signal Alarm (1982); Bus Stop (1983); The Primitive (1985); The Other Shore (1986); Soul Mountain (1989); The Voice of the Individual (1995); and One Man's Bible (autobiography, 2000).

2001

Sir Vidiadhar Surajprasad "V. S." Naipaul

(May 17, 1932...

B. Chaganas, Trinidad

A Trinidadian novelist and essayist of Indio-Trinidadian descent. He has been called 'a master of modern English prose.' He was married to Patricia Ann Hale from 1955 until her death in 1996. She served as first reader, editor, and critic of his writings. Naipaul dedicated his A House for Mr. Biswas to her.

"for having united perceptive narrative and incorruptible scrutiny in works that compel us to see the presence of suppressed histories"

He has been awarded numerous literary prizes, including the John Llewellyn Prize (1958); Somerset Maugham Award (1960); the Booker Prize (1971); and the Hawthornden Prize (1964). The Times ranked him 7th on their list of 'the 50 greatest British writers since 1945'.

He is Joseph Conrad's heir as the annalist of the destinies of empires in the moral sense: what they do to human beings. His novels deal with individuals who have become estranged from society and spend their lives searching for their identities. The Mystic Masseur (1957), his first novel, is a satire about the life of the poor in Trinidad. A House for Mr. Biswas (1961) and A Bend in the River (1979) are his best-known novels. He has also written travel books in which he describes both physical and emotional journeys. An Area of Darkness (1964) records his impressions on a trip through India.

His works: The Mystic Masseur, 1957 (film version The Mystic Masseur, 2002); Suffrage of Elvira (1958); Miguel Street (1959); The Enigma of Arrival (1987); The Way of the World (1994); India: A Wounded Civilization (1977); Finding the Center (1984); India: A Million Mutinies (1990); The Writer and the World: essays (2002); and A Writer's People: Ways of Looking and Feeling (2007).

2002

Imre Kertész

(November 9, 1929....

B. Budapest, Hungary

Hungarian Jewish author, Holocaust Concentration Camp Survivor.

"for writing that upholds the fragile experience of the individual against the arbitrariness of history"

At the age of 14 he was deported with other Hungarian Jews during World War II to the Auschwitz concentration camp in 1944. He was liberated from the camp in 1945. After the war he found work at Budapest Newspaper, Világos, but in 1951 he was forced out because of the Communist takeover. He joined the military for two years and has since made a living translating German authors into Hungarian. Among his works in 1975 is novel entitled Faithless, based on his experience in the Nazi camp. He initially found little appreciation for his writing in Hungary and moved to Germany. He continues to write in Hungarian and submitted his works to publishers in Hungary. In his semiautobiographical novel he has analyzed the experience of individual during barbaric times, specially exemplified in Holocaust. In his youth he experienced the horrors of the Nazi system. Germans occupied Hungary in 1944 and began exterminating Jews and Gypsies. He started translating German works into Hungarian and did not publish another novel until the late 1980s. A film based on his novel Faithlessness was made in Hungary in 2005 for which he wrote the script. The film was released at various dates throughout the world in 2005 and 2006. He is a controversial figure within Hungary, specially because he lives in Germany.

Other works: Fiasco (1988); Kaddish for a Child Not Born (1977). (The Kaddish is a Jewish prayer said in the memory of the diseased); The Pathfinder (1977); The English Play (1991); and Galley Dairy (1992).

2003

John Maxwell "J. M." Coetzee

Born: John Michael Coetzee

(February 9, 1940...

B. Cape Town, South Africa

South African author and academic, now an Australian citizen living in South Australia. He is also a novelist, literary critic as well as a translator.

"who in innumerable guises portrays the surprising involvement of the outsider"

He spent most of his early childhood in Cape Town and in Worcester in Cape Province as recounted in his fictionalized memoir, Boyhood (1997). The family spoke English at home, but Coetzee spoke Afrikaans with other relatives. On March 6, 2006 he became an Australian Citizen. He attended St. Joseph's College, a Catholic school in the Cape Town suburbs of Rondebosch, and later studied mathematics and English at the University of Cape Town, receiving his Bachelor of Arts with Honors in 1960 and his Bachelor of Arts with Honors in mathematics in 1961 . In early 1960s he relocated to London, where he worked for a time in IBM as a computer programmer, and in 1963 he was awarded a Master of Arts degree from UCT for a dissertation on the novels of Ford Madox Ford. He received a Ph.D. in linguistic at the University of Texas. He is a man of almost monkish self-discipline and dedication. He does not drink, smoke or eat meat. He cycles vast distances to keep fit.

Awards: He was awarded James Tait Black Memorial Prize for his novel Waiting for the Barbarians, and he is three times winner of CNA Prize. Age of Iron was awarded the Sunday Express Book of the Year Award.

Works: Dusklands (1974); In the Heart of the Country (1977); Waiting for the Barbarians (1980); Foe (1986); Age of Iron (1990); The Master of Petersburg (1994); Disgrace (1999); and Slow Man (2005).

2004

Elfriede Jelinek

(October 20, 1946...

B. Mürzzuschlag, Styria, Austria

Austrian feminist playwright and novelist.

Jelinek means "Little deer in Czech."

"for her musical flow of voices and counter-voices in novels and plays that, with extraordinary linguistic zeal reveal the absurdity of society's clichés and their subjugating power"

Her father, a chemist of Jewish-Czech origin managed to avoid persecution during World War II by working in strategically important industrial production. At the early age, she was instructed in piano, organ and recorder and went on to study composition at the Vienna Conservatory. She studied at the Vienna Conservatory, where she graduated with an organist diploma. She also studied art history and drama at the University of Vienna, but she had to discontinue her studies due to an anxiety disorder. She started with writing poetry at a young age. She made her literary debut with the collection Lisas Schatten (1967). Through contact with the student movement, her writing took a socially critical direction. She was a member of Austria's Communist Party from 1974 to 1991. She became a household name during the 1990s due to her vociferous clash with Jörg Haider's far-right Freedom Party. She has won many distinguished prizes: Georg Büchner Prize (1998); the Mülheim Dramatists Prize (2002, 2004); The Franz Kafka Prize (2004). In her later work, Jelinek has somewhat abandoned female issues to focus her energy on social criticism in general, and Austria's difficulties in admitting to its Nazi past in particular.

Some of her works: Die Ausgesperrten (1980); Die Kinder der Toten (1995); The Piano Teacher (1988); Women as Lovers (1994); Lust (1989); and Greed (2000).

2005

Harold Pinter

(October 10, 1930-December 24, 2008)

B. Kackney, London, England

D. West London, England

English playwright, screen writer, actor, director, poet, author, and political activist.

He received 20 honorary degrees and numerous other prizes and awards. Writing period: 1947-2008

"who in his plays uncovers the precipice under every day prattle and forces entry into oppression's closed rooms"

A sense of life's meaningfulness, an atmosphere of menace, and comic elements characterized his work. He studied briefly at the Royal Academy of Dramatic art. He began his theatrical career as an actor, touring Ireland and the English provinces for nine years under the stage name of David Baron. An avid reader of fiction and poetry, he experimented in both these forms, but the production of his first play, The Room, in 1957 at the University of Bristol began his development as a writer for the stage. He also achieved success as a director and as a film writer, notably for the screenplays for The Servant, The Pumpkin Eater, and Accident. All of Pinter's plays benefit from his experience as an actor and director—they emphasize not the literary moment but a carefully calculated dramatic one.   His best-known plays include The Birthday Party (1957), The Caretaker (1959), and Betrayal (1981). He directed almost 50 stage, television, and film productions and acted extensively in radio, stage, television production of his own and others' works. At the time of his death, he was considered by many "the most influential and imitated dramatist of his generation" and "one of the most influential British playwrights of modern times."

Some of his other works: The Dumb Writer (1957); No Man's Land (1975); Family Voices (1981); Poems and Prose (1949-77) was published 1n 1979.

2006

Ferit Orhan Pamuk

(June 7, 1952…

B. Istanbul, Turkey

Turkish novelist, and professor of Comparative Literature and Writing at Columbia University.

"who in quest for the melancholic soul of his native city has discovered new symbols for the clash and interlacing of cultures"

One of Turkey's most prominent novelists, his work has sold over seven million books in more than 50 languages, making him the country's best-selling writer. He is the recipient of numerous literary awards. He is the first Turkish citizen to be awarded Nobel Prize. He was educated at Robert College secondary school in Istanbul and went on to study architecture at the University of Istanbul in 1976. He left the architecture school after three years, however, to become a full-time writer and graduated from the Institute of Journalism at the University of Istanbul in 1976. He is a Muslim, and he describes himself as cultural one who associates the historical and cultural identification with the religion. In 2006 Pamuk returned to the United States to take up a position as a visiting professor at Columbia. In May 2007 he was among the jury members at the Cannes Film Festival. Popular success took a bit longer to come to Pamuk, but his 1990 novel Kara Kitap (The Black Book) became one of the most controversial and popular readings in Turkish literature, due to its complexity and richness. He has won numerous awards from 1979 to present. He also won the Orhan Kemal Novel Prize (1983).

His works: Darkness and Light (1979); The White Castle (1991); The New Life (1997); My Name is Red (2001); Snow (2004); Istanbul: Memories of a City (2005); Sessiz Ev (The Silent House, 1983); The Museum of Innocence (2009).

2007

Doris May Lessing

Pen name: Jane Somers

(October 22, 1919-November 17, 2013)

B. Kermanshah, Iran

D. London England

She is the eleventh woman to win the Nobel Prize in its 108 year history, and also the oldest person ever to win the literary award. She was awarded the David Cohen Prize for a lifetime's achievement in British Literature. In 2008, The Times ranked her fifth on the List of 50 greatest British writers since 1945.

"that epicist of the female experience, who with skepticism, fire and visionary power has subjected a divided civilization to scrutiny"

She was educated at the Dominican Convent High School. She has used her fiction to explore such important contemporary themes as political commitment, the male-female dynamic on its most fundamental level, women's search for identity, and the relationships between the artist and his or her work. She is probably best known for her long, experimental novel (The Golden Notebook, 1962), focusing on the lives of two talented professional women.

Although she has lived in England since 1949, she was born in Iran and brought up in Rhodesia (now Zimbabwe), the setting for her first novel, The Grass is Singing (1950). Between 1952 and 1962 she published 5 novels, collectively titled The Children of Violence. She has won numerous awards from 1954 to 2002: Somerset Maugham Award (1954); Palmero Prize (1987); Order of the Companions of Honor (1999); and S.T. Dupont Golden PEN Award (2002).

Works: The Memoirs of Survivor (1974); Canopus in Argos (1979); The Good Terrorist (1985); The Fifth Child (1988); Love, Again (1990); The Sweetest Dream (2001); The Cleft (2007); and Alfred and Emily (2008).

2008

Jean-Marie Gustave Le Clézio

(April 13, 1940...

B. Riviera, Nice, France

French author and professor, author of over 40 works.

"author of new departures, poetic adventure and sensual ecstasy, explorer of a humanity beyond and below the reigning civilization"

He was awarded the 1963 Prix Renaudot for his novel Le Procès-Verbal. Both his parents had strong family connections with the former French colony, Mauritius. After completing his secondary education, he studied English at Bristol University in 1958-59 and completed undergraduate degree in Nice in 1963. He took a master's degree at the University of Aix-en-Provence in 1964. He has taught at the universities in Bangkok, Mexico City, Boston, Austin and Albuquerque among other places. After several years spent in London and Bristol, he moved to The United States to work as a teacher. During 1967 he served in the French military in Thailand, but was quickly expelled from the country for protesting against child prostitution and was sent to Mexico City to finish his military obligation. A frequent visitor to South Korea, he taught French and literature at Ewha Womans University in Seoul during the 2007 academic year. He has been writing since age 7, his first book was a book about the sea. He achieved very early success at age 23. Since then he has published more than 36 books, including short stories, novels, essays, and several children's books.

His works: Le Livre des fuites (The Book of Flights: An Adventure Story, 1969); La Guerre (War, 1970); Poisson d'or (Fish of Gold, 1996); Lullaby (1980); Ballaciner, 2007); The Flood (1967); Terra Amata (1969); and Trois Villes saintes (Three Holy Cities, 1980).

Awards: Prix littéraire Valery-Larbaud for his complete works (1972).

2009

Herta Müller

(August 7, 1953...

B. Nițchidorf, Timiș County, Romania

Romanian–born German novelist, poet, and essayist noted for her works depicting the effects of violence, cruelty, and terror usually in the setting of Communist Romania under the repressive Nicolae Ceaușescu regime which she experienced herself.

"who with the concentration of poetry and the frankness of prose, depicts the landscape of the dispossessed"

She has been an internationally well-known author since the early 1990s, and her works have been translated into more than 20 languages. She has received over 20 awards, including the 1994 Kleist Prize, the 1995 Aristeion Prize, 1998 International IMPAC Dublin Literary Award, and the 2009 Franz Werfel Human Rights Award. In 2009, her first book Niederungen (Nadris), was published in Romania in German in 1982, in a state-censored version. Müller enjoyed the greatest international success of her career.

Her novel Atemschaukel, published in English (The Hunger Angel) was nominated for the Deutscher (German Book Prize) and won the Franc Werfel Human Right. It portrays the deportation of Romania's German minority to Stalinist Soviet Gulag during the Soviet occupation of Romania for use as forced labor.

Her works: Druckender Tango (Oppressive Tango, 1994); Barfüßiger Februar (Barefoot February, Berlin, 1987); Hunger Und Seide (Hunger and Silk, Hamburg, 1995); Der Teufel Sitzt im Spiegel (The Devil is Sitting in the Mirror, Berlin, 1999); and Angekommen wie nicht da (Arrived as If Not There, 1994).

Some other prizes: Aspekte Literature Prize, 1985; Rauris Literature Prize, 1985; Critical Prize for Literature, 1993; Literature Prize of Graz, 1997; Berlin Literature Prize, 2009; and Hofmann von Fallersleben Prize, 2010.

2010

Jorge Mario Pedro Vargas Llosa

First Marquis of Vargas Llosa

(March 28 1936...

B. Arequipa, Arequipa, Peru

He is a Peruvian-Spanish writer, politician, journalist, and essayist.

"for his cartography of structures of power and his trenchant images of the individual's resistance, revolt, and defeat"

While in Lima, he studied at Colegio la Salle, a Christian middle school (1947-49). In 1953, he enrolled in Lima's National University of San Marcos to study law and literature. Upon his graduation in 1958, he received a scholarship to study at the Complutense University of Madrid in Spain. He is one of the Latin America's most significant novelists and essayist, and one of the leading authors of his generation. Some critics consider him to have had a larger international impact and worldwide audience than any other Latin America Boom. He rose to fame in the 1960s with novels such as The Time of the Hero (La ciudad y Las Perros, literally the City and the Dogs, 1963/1966); The Green House (La casa Verde, 1968/1968); and the monumental Conversation in the Cathedral (Conversación en la Catedral, 1969/75). His novels include comedies, murder mysteries, historical novels, and political thrillers. Several such as Captain Pantoja and the Special Service (1973/1978) and Aunt Julia and the Scriptwriter (1977/ 82), have been adapted as feature films. Like many of Latin American authors, Vargas has been politically active throughout his career.

Selected works: Los jefes, 1959 (The Cubs and Other Stories, 1979); La tia Julia y el escribidor, 1977 (Aunt Julia and the Scriptwriter, 1982); La fiesta del chivo, 2000 (The Feast of the Goat, 2002); El sueño del celto, 2010 (The Dream of the Celt, 2010).

2011

Tomas Gösta Tranströmer

(April 15, 1931...

B. Stockholm, Sweden

He is a Swedish poet, psychologist and translator. His poems capture the long Swedish winters, the rhythm of the oceans and the palpable, atmospheric beauty of the nature.

"because through his condensed, translucent images, he gives us fresh access to reality"

His works is also characterized by a sense of mystery and wonder underlying the routine of everyday life, a quality which often give his poems a religious dimension. He is acclaimed as one of the most important Scandinavian writers since the Second World War. His poetry has been translated into 60 languages. He received his secondary education at the Södra Latin School in Stockholm.

He continued his education at Stockholm University, graduating as a psychologist in 1956 with additional studies in history, religion and literature. An English translation by Robin Fulton of his entire body of work, New Collected Poems, was published in the UK. in 1987 and expanded in 1997. The Syrian poet Adunis helped spread Tranströmer's fame in the Arab world. Besides being a brilliant writer, he has also a successful career as a respected psychologist behind him. He suffered a stroke in 1990 that left him partially paralyzed and unable to speak; however he would continue to write and publish poetry through the early 2000s.

Selected works: 17 Poems (17 dikters), Bonniers, 1954; Secrets in the Way (Hemligheter på vägen) Bonnier, 1958; The Half-Finished Heaven (Den halvfärdiga himlen) Bonnier, 1962; Bells and Tracks (Klanger och spår) Bonnier, 1966.

Awards and honors: Petrarca-Preis (Germany, 1981); Jan Smerk Award (Slovakia, 1998); and Struga Poetry Evenings Golden Wreath, Macedonia, 2003.

2012

Guan Moye, Pen name: Mo Yan

(Feb 17, 1955...

B. Gaomi, Shandong, China

Chinese novelist and short story writer.

"who with hallucinatory realism merges folk tales, history and the cotemporary"

He is best known to Western readers for his 1987 novel Sorghum Clan. Mo was 11 years old when the Cultural Revolution was launched, at which time he left school to work as a farmer. During this period, which coincided with succession of political campaigns from the Great Leap Forward to the Cultural Revolution. His access to literature was largely limited to the novels in the socialist realist style under Mao Zedong, which centered largely on the themes of class struggle and conflict. At the close of the Cultural Revolution in 1976, Mo enlisted in the People's Liberation Army (PLA), and began writing while he was still a soldier. He is the first non-dissident Chinese national to win a Nobel Prize, and his award thus celebrated as a moment of international recognition that has long eluded China. In 1984 he received a literary award from the PLA Magazine, and at this year began attending the Military Art Academy, where he first adopted the pen name Mo Yan. He published his first novella A Transparent Radish in 1984, and released Red Sorghum in 1986, launching his career as a nationally recognized novelist. In 1991 he obtained a master's degree in literature from Beijing Normal University. His first novel was Falling Rain on a Spring Night (1981). Several of his novels were translated into English by Howard Goldblatt, professor of East Asian languages and literature at the University of Notre Dame.

Selected works: The Garlic Ballads (1988, English, 1995); The Breasts and Wide Hips (1995, 2005); Falling Rain on a Spring Night, 1981; Life and Death Are Wearing Me Out (2008); and Meeting the Masters (1990-2005).

2013

Alice Ann Munro (Laidlaw)

(July 10, 1931…

B. Wingham, Ontario, Canada

Canadian author writing in English. She is the first Canadian to receive the Nobel Prize.

" master of the contemporary short story."

The focus of her fiction is her native Horn County in southwestern Ontario. Her "accessible, moving stories" explore human complexities in a seemingly effortless style.

Munro's writing has established her as "one of our greatest contemporary writers of fiction." Munro began writing as a teenager, publishing her first story, "The Dimensions of a Shadow" in 1950 while studying English and journalism at the University of Western Ontario. During this period she worked as a waitress, tobacco picker, and a library clerk.

In 1951, she left the university, where she had been majoring in English since 1949. Her highly acclaimed first collection of stories, Dance of the Happy Shades (1968), won the Governor's General Award, Canada's highest literary award. Her stories have appeared frequently in publications such as The New Yorker, The Atlantic Monthly, Grand Street, Mademoiselle, and The Paris Review. Munro's prose deals with the ambiguities of life: "ironic and serious at the same time." Her stories have been said to "embed more than announce, reveal more than parade."

Works: Lives of Girls and Women (1971); Who Do You Think You Are? (1978) ; The Progress of Love (1986); Open Secrets (1994); Runaway (2004); The View from Castle Rock (2006); Too Much Happiness (2009); and Dear Life (2012).

Awards: Governor General's Literary Award for English language fiction (1968, 1978, 1986); Merion Engel Award (1986); and Trillium Book Award (19991, 1999, 2013).

2014

Jean Patrick Modiano

(July 30, 1945...

B. Boulogne-Billancourt, France

"for the art of memory with which he has evoked and uncovered the life-world of the occupation"

He was born two months after World War II to a father with Jewish-Italian origin and Belgian actress mother. He has made a lifelong study of the Nazi occupation and its effects on his country. Jewishness, the Nazi occupation and loss of identity are the recurrent themes in his novels.

Modiano is the 107th recipient of the prize and the 11th French to win the prestigious 1.1 million dollar award. Modiano gained popularity in the late 1060s and has about 30 works to his name, mostly novel, though he also writes movie scripts and children's books. Modiano's childhood took place in a unique atmosphere. He was first brought up by his maternal grandparents who taught him Flemish, his first language. He completed his secondary education by government aid, being able to put up between the absence of his father and his mother's frequent tours.

He studied at the École du Montcel primary school in Jouy-en-Josas, at the Collège Saint-Joseph, and then at the Lycèe Henri-IV high school in Paris, but he did not continue his higher education. The turning point in Modiano's life came when he met Raymond Queneau, French author of Zazie dans le Métro. He was the person who introduced the young French lad to the world of literature. Several of his books have been translated into various languages.

Works: La Ronde de nuit, 1969 (Night Rounds, 1971); Villa triste (1975); Remise de Peine (1988); Voyage de noces, 1990 (Honeymoon Trip, 1992); Dora Bruder (1997); Accident nocturne (2003); and L'Herbe de nuit (2012).

Awards: Prix Goncourt (for lifetime achievement, 1978); Prix mondial Cino del Duca (2010) and Austrian State Prize for European Literature (2012).

Glossary

A

Agrigneto: a city on the Southern coast of Sicily, Italy.

Academie française (French Academy): is the pre-eminent French learned body on matters pertaining to the French language.

Abbaye de St. Maurice: a historical building in Saint Maurice.

Andalusia: is the most populous and the second largest in area of the autonomous communities in Spain.

Algeria (The People's Democratic Republic of Algeria): is a country in North Africa on the Mediterranean Coast.

Saoi of Absodána: members of Absodána may receive the honor of saoi (wise one, master).

Salvator Guillermo Allende Gossens (June 26, 1908-Sept. 11, 1973) was a Chilean physician and politician, as the first Marxist to become the president of Latin America through open elections.

Albania (The Republic of Albania) is a country in Southeastern Europe.

Athens: is the capital and largest city of Greek islands.

Arcataca (Cataca): is a municipality located in the department of Magdalena in Colombia's Caribbean Region.

The University of Anglia: is a public research University based on Norwich, United Kingdom.

Abikuta: is the largest and capital of Ogun State in southeast Nigeria.

Anna Akhmatova (June 23, 1889-March 5, 1966) Russian modernist poet.

Al-Hilal: was a weekly Urdu language newspaper established by the Indian leader Maulana Abul Kalam Azad.

Al-Ahram (the pyramids): founded in 1875, is the most widely circulating Egyptian daily newspaper.

Albany: north of city of New York sits on the west bank of the Hudson River.

Azinhoga: is a small village near Golegã, Ribatejo, Portugal.

Auschwits: is a town in southwest Poland: the site of Nazi death camp during World War II.

Australia: a continent in southeast of Asia, between the Indian and Pacific Oceans.

Aix-en-Provence (Aix): is a city-commune in south France.

Albuquerque: is the largest city in the U.S. state of New Mexico.

Aristerion prize: is a European literary annual prize. It is given to authors for significant contributors to contemporary European literature.

Arequipa: is the capital and largest city of the province of Arequipa and the seat of the Constitutional Court of the "Legal Capital of Peru".

B

Blogna: is the largest city and the capital of Emilia-Romagna Region in Northern Italy.

Berlin: is the capital and the largest city of Germany.

Bonn: is the largest city of the German state of Bavaria.

Breslau: in 1335, together with almost all Silesia, was incorporated into the Kingdom of Bohemia, then a part of Holy Roman Empire.

Bengali: an Indo-American language spoken in Bangladesh.

Ludwig Van Beethoven (17 Dec. 1770-26 March 1827, born in Bonn) German composer and pianist.

Brahma: in Hinduism, Brahma is frequently viewed as the creator or creative aspect of God, responsible for originating of each endless circle of existence recognized in classical Hinduism.

Brahman (the neuter form of Brahma) is the name given to the fundamental principal of the universe in the Vedant, the teachings of Upanishads, and philosophies stemming from them.

George Morris Cohen Brandes (Feb. 4, 1842-Feb. 19, 1927) was a Danish critic and scholar who had great influence on Scandinavian and European literature.

Buddhism: is a religion indigenous to the Indian subcontinent that encompasses a variety of traditions, beliefs, and practices largely based on teachings attributed to Siddharta Guatama, who is commonly known as the Buddha, meaning "the awakened one."

Bern: the city of Bern or Berne is the Bundesstadt (federal city) of Switzerland.

Ethel Barrymore (Aug. 15, 1879-June 18, 1959): American actress and member the family of actors.

Boston: is the capital and largest city of the U.S. state of Massachusetts.

Belleme: is a commune in the Orme department in northwestern France.

The Boxer Uprising (Rebellion): began at the turn of the 20th century in the area of Beijing, China.

Byhalia: is a town in the Marshall County, Mississippi, U.S.A.

Bordeaux: is a port city on the Garrone River in the Gironde department in southwestern France.

Blenheim: is a village and civil parish within the West Oxfordshire district north of Oxford, Oxfordshire, England.

Bosnia and Herzegovina (Bosnia): is a country in Southwestern Europe.

Belgrad: is the capital and the largest city of Serbia.

Batume: is a seaside city on the Black Sea coast and the capital of Adjara.

Simon de Beauvoir (9 Jan. 1908-14 April 1986): was a French writer, intellectual, existentialist philosopher, political activist, feminist, and social theorist.

Boguchar: is a town and the administrative center of Bogucharsky District of Vorunezh Oblast, Russia.

Bolsheviks: were a faction of the Marxist Russian Social Democratic Labor Party.

Buczacz (Buchach): is a city located on the Strypa River on Tempopil Oblast of western Ukraine.

The Bialik Prize: is an annual literary prize given by the municipality of Tel Aviv, Israel.

Samuel Beckett (Apr. 13, 1906-Dec. 22, 1989): was an Irish advant-grade novelist, playwright, theatre director, and poet.

The Georg Büchner Prize: is the most important prize in Germany.

Boden: is a locality and the seat of Boden Municipality in Norbotten County, Sweden.

Brookline: is a suburban town in Norfolk County, Massachusetts, U.S.A.

The University of Berkeley: is a public research university located in Berkeley, California, U.S.A.

Barcelona: is the capital of Catalonia and the second largest city in Spain.

Boston Playwrights' Theatre: award winning professional theatre, founded in 1981 to promote new plays.

Belaghy: is a village in County Londonderry, Ireland.

Belfast (mouth of the sandbanks): is the largest city of Northern Ireland.

Brera Art Academy: is a public academic institution in Milan, Italy.

Bertold Brecht (Feb. 10, 1898-Aug. 14, 1956) German poet, playwright, theatre director, and Marxist.

Bangnolet: is a commune in the eastern suburbs of Paris, France.

Booker Prize: is an annual British literary award sponsored by the business firm Booker McConnell and administered by the National Book League, was instituted in 1968.

Budapest: is the capital and the largest city in Hungary and the largest in East-Central Europe.

Bristol: is the largest city in southwestern English. It is an international seaport on Avon River.

Basel or Basle: is Switzerland's 3rd most populous city, located where the Swiss, French and German borders meet.

Bangkok: is the capital and the most populous city in Thailand.

C

Châtenay-Malabry: is a commune in the southwestern Paris, France.

Charlottenburg: is an affluent locality of Berlin within the borough of Charlottenburg-Wilmersdorf.

Calcutta: is a city and port in the eastern India and the capital of West Bengal state.

Olshammar: is a locality situated in Askersund Municipality, Örebro, Sweden. **Copenhagen**: is the capital of Denmark on the east coast of Zealand.

Clermont-Ferrand: is a city and commune of France in Auvergne region, France.

Joseph Conrad (Dec. 3, 1852-Aug. 3, 1924): was a Polish author who wrote in English after settling in England.

The Count of Monte Cristo: is an adventure novel by French author Alexandre Dumas.

Confucian: of, relating to, or characteristic of Confucius, his teachings, or his followers.

Christian II of Denmark (July 1, 1481-Jan. 25, 1559) reigned as King of Denmark and Norway (1913-1923) and Sweden (1520-1521).

Confucius (551-479 B.C.): was a Chinese teacher, editor, philosopher, of the Spring and Autumn period of Chinese history.

Cimbrean: refers to any several local Upper German varieties spoken in northeastern Italy.

Lord Landorph Henry-Spencer Churchill (Feb. 13, 1849- Jan. 24, 1895) was a British statesman and the 3rd son of the Duke of Marlborough.

Clervaux: is a commune and town in northern Luxembourg, administrative capital of the canton of Clervaux.

Hermann Cohen (Jul. 4, 1842-Apr. 4, 1918) German-Jewish philosopher, one of the founders of the Marburg School of Neo-Kantism.

Paul Claudel (6 Aug. 1868-23 Feb. 1955) French poet, dramatist and diplomat.

Croatia (The Republic of Croatia) is a unitary democratic parliamentary republic at the crossroads of Central Europe.

Crete: is the largest and the most populous of the Greek islands.

Robert Capa (Oct. 22, 1913-May 25, 1954) was a Hungarian combat photographer photojournalist who covered 5 different wars.

Manuel José Estrada Cabrera (21 Nov. 1857-24 Sept. 1924) was President of Cuba from Feb. 8, 1898 to Apr. 15, 1920.

Chile (The Republic of Chile) is a South American country in South West America on the Pacific Coast.

Spanish Civil War (17 Jul. 1936-Apr. 1, 1939) begins as a revolt by right-wing by Spanish military officers in Spanish Morocco and spreads to mainland Spain.

Cheltenham College: is a co-educational independent school, located in Cheltenham, Gloucestershire, England.

Castle Hill: is a suburb in the north-west of Sydney, in the state of New South Wales, Australia.

Corriere de la Cera (Evening Courier) Italian daily newspaper.

Chicago: a city in Northeast Illinois, on Lake Michigan.

Colombia (Republic of Colombia) is a unitary constitutional republic comprising 32 departments.

Cornwall: is a unitary authority and ceremonial county of England.

Columb Minor: is a village on the north coast of Cornwall, England.

Czechoslovakia: was a sovereign state in Central Europe that existed from October 1918, when it declared its independence from the Astro-Hungarian Empire.

Chapter 77: was an informal civic initiative in communist Czechoslovakia from 1976 to 1992.

Cairo: is the capital of Egypt and the largest city in the Arab world and Africa.

Juan Carlos (B. Jan. 5, 1938): king of Spain (Nov. 22, 1975).

Gerardo Diego Cendoya (October 3, 1896-July 8, 1987) Spanish poet, a member of Generation 27.

Castries: is the capital and the largest city of Saint Lucia.

Francis Coheen (Aug. 15, 1919-Mar. 31, 2008) American academic of Princeton University and U.S. Ambassador to India.

Castledowson: is a village in County Londonderry, Northern Island.

Columb's College: is a Roman Catholic boy's grammar school in Derry, Northern Island.

Changuanas: the borough of Changuanas is the largest and fastest-growing town in Trinidad and Tobago.

Cape Town: is the capital and the second-most populated city in South Africa.

The Province of the Cape of Good Hope (Cape Town Province) was a province in Union of South Africa.

Cannes Film Festival: the Cannes International Film Festival is an annual Film Festival held in Cannes, France.

The David Cohen Prize (Established in 1993): is a biennial British literary award given to writers, novelist, short story writers, essayist or dramatists in recognition of the entire body of work, written in English.

Clamecy: is a commune in the Nièvre department in central France.

Nicolae Ceauşescu (Jan. 25, 1918-Dec. 25, 1989) Romanian

politician. He was General Secretary of the Romanian Communist Party from 1965 to 1989, and as such the country's last Communist leader.

D

Léon Dierx (March 31, 1858-June 12, 1912) was a French poet born in the island of La Reunion.

Dublin: is the capital of the Republic of Ireland, in the East part, on the Irish Sea.

Dreyfus Affair: was a political scandal that divided France from its inception in 1894 until its resolution in 1906.

Danby: is a town in Rutland County, Vermont, U.S.A.

Charles de Gaule (Charles André Joseph Marie de Gaule) (Nov. 22, 1890-Nov. 9, 1870) was a French general and statesman who led the French Forces during World War II.

Diario de Noticias: is a Portuguese daily national newspaper.

Danzig Trilogy: is a series of novels or novellas by German author Günter Grass.

Düsseldorf: is the capital city of the German state of North Rhine-Westphalia.

Dominican Republic: is a nation on the island of Hispaniola part of the Greater Antilles archipelago in the Caribbean region.

Dupont Golden PEN Award: is a literary award established in 1993 by English PEN given annually to a British Writer for "A Lifetime Distinguished Service to Literature."

E

Enniskillen: is a town and civil parish in County Fermanagh, Northern Ireland.

Ewha Woman's University: is a private women's university in central Seoul, South Korea.

F

Foxrock: is a suburb of Dublin, Ireland.

Le Figaro: is a French newspaper founded in 1827 and published in Paris.

Frankfurt (Frankfurt am Main): is a city in West Germany on the Main River.

King Fuad (Fouad) (March 26, 1868-Apr. 28, 1936) was the Sultan and later the King of Egypt and Sudan Sovereign of Nubia, Kordofan, and Darfur.

Francisco Franco y Bahamonde (Dec. 4, 1892-Nov. 20, 1975) was a Spanish military leader and statesman who ruled as the dictator of Spain from 1936 until his death.

Ford Madox Ford (Hermann Hueffer) (Dec. 17, 1873-June 26, 1939) English novelist, poet, critic, and educator.

Robin Fulton (18 Aug. 1937...) Scottish poet and translator. He was born on the Isle of Arran. He has lived in Stavangar, Norway, since 1973 working as a university lecturer.

G

Charles Gounad (June 17, 1818-Oct. 17, 1899) French composer well known for Ave Maria as well as his opera Faust.

Johan Wolfgang von Goethe (Aug. 28, 1749-March 22, 1832) German writer, artist and politician.

Gottingen: is a university town in Lower Saxony, Germany.

Ghent: is a city and municipality located in the Flemish region of Belgium.

Grimstad: is a town and municipality in Aus-Agder county, Norway.

Isabella Augusta, Lady Gregory (15 March, 1852-22 May, 1932) Irish dramatist, folklorist and theatre manager.

Goppingen: is the town in southern Germany, part of the Stuttgart Region of Baden-Württemberg.

Gottfried-Keller-Preis: is one of the oldest literary awards of Switzerland.

Genoa: is the capital of Liguria and is the 6th largest city of Italy.

Guadeloupe: is a Caribbean island in the Leeward Islands, in the Lesser Antilles.

Graz: is the second largest city in Austria and the capital of the federal state of Styria.

Galicia: is an autonomous community in northwestern Spain.

Guatemala (the Republic of Guatemala): is a country in North Central America bordered by Mexico to the north and west.

Guatemala City: is the capital and largest city of Guatemala and Central America.

Greece: officially the Hellenic Republic, and known since ancient times as Hellas, is a country in Southeast Europe.

Gar du Nord (North Station): is one of the 6 large terminus railway stations SNCF mainline network for Paris, France.

Guggenheim fellowships are grants that have been awarded since 1925 by the John Simon Guggenheim Memorial Foundation to those who have demonstrated exceptional capacity.

Ganzhou (Kanchow): is a prefecture city in southern Jangxi Province, China.

Generation of 1936: is the name given to a group of Spanish artists, writers, poets and playwrights who were working about the time of Spanish Civil War.

Gangkou District: is a district of Guangxi, China.

Gulag: the Gulag was the Soviet Union government agency that administered the main Soviet forced labor camp systems during the Stalin era (1930s-1950s).

Gaomi: is a county-level city of Shandong Province, People's Republic of China.

The Great Leap Forward of People's Republic of China: was an economic and social campaign by the Communist Party of China.

Howard Goldblatt (Born in 1939...) was a research professor of Chinese at the University of Notre Dame from 2002 to 2011 and as a translator of numerous works of contemporary Chinese fiction.

H

Hosé-Maria de Heredia (Nov.22, 1842-Oct 3, 1905) A Cuban-born French poet. He was the 15th member elected for seat 4 of the Académie française (French Academy) in 1894.

Holstein: is the region between the rivers Elbe and Eider. It is part of Schlewig-Holstein, the northernmost state of Germany.

Heinrich Heine (Dec. 13, 1797-Feb. 17, 1856): was one of the most significant poets of the 19th century.

Hanover (Hannover): on the river Leine, is the capital of the federal state of Lower Saxony, Germany.

Hedersler grammar school: a grammar school is one of the several different kinds of school in the history of education in the United Kingdom and some other English-speaking countries.

Heidleburg: is a city in southwest Germany and the fifth largest city in the State of Baden-Württemberg.

Hertfordshire: was the area assigned to a fortress constructed at Hertford under the rule of Edward the Elder in 963.

Harrow College: is the largest college in London Borough of Harrow.

Hillsboro: is a town in Pocahontas County, West Virginia, U.S.A.

Hämeenkyrö: is a municipality located in the province of Western Finland and is part of the Prikanmaa region.

Helsinki: is the capital of Finland, on the sea coast. It is in the region of Uusimaa, located in southern Finland.

Himmerland: is a peninsula in northeastern Jutland, Denmark.

Hampstead: is one of the three towns in Nassau County, New York, U.S.A.

Hyde Park: is one of the largest parks in central London, and one of London's 8 Royal Parks.

Nicolai Hartmann (Feb. 20, 1882-Oct. 9, 1950) is one of the leading German philosophers.

Heraklion (Heraclion, Iraklion) is the largest city and the administrative capital of the island of Crete, Greece.

Hoard University: is a federally chartered, coeducational, nonsectarian, historically black university in Washington D.C., U.S.A.

Stephen William Hawking (Born Jan. 8, 1942…) is a British theoretical physicist, cosmologist, author and Director of research at the Centre for Theoretical Cosmology within the University of Cambridge.

Hawthornden Prize: is a British literary award that was established in 1919 by Alice Warrender. Authors are awarded on the quality of their "imaginative literature."

The Holocaust: the systematic mass slaughter of European Jews in Nazi concentration camps during World War II.

Jorg Haider (Jan. 26, 1950-Oct. 11, 2008) was an Austrian politician and the leader of Austrian Freedom Party.

Hackney: is the London Borough located in east of the city of London.

I

Henrik Ibsen (March. 20, 1828-May 23, 1906): was a major 19th century novelist, playwright, the theatre director and poet.

Illinois: is a state in the Midwestern U.S.A.

Idaho: is a mountainous state with an area larger than that all of New England.

Imperia: is a coastal city and commune in the region of Liguria, Italy.

Israel (the State of Israel): is a parliamentary democracy in the Middle

East, on the southeastern shore of Mediterranean Sea.

Istanbul: is the largest city in Turkey, consisting the country's economic, cultural, and historical heart.

Iran: is the most populous and the second-largest country in the Middle East, and a major exporter of oil.

IMPAC International, Dublin literary award: is given for new works on the high literary merit in the English language.

Iraq (the Republic of Iraq): is a country in Western Asia.

University of Ibadan: is the oldest Nigerian university in western Nigeria.

J

Jena: is a university city in central Germany University town and the 2nd largest city in Thuringia.

Jurisprudence: the science and philosophy of law.

Jerusalem: the capital of Israel and one of the oldest cities in the world.

Jutland: historically called Cimbria, is the name of the peninsula that juts out in the Northern Europe.

Carl Gostav Jung (Jul. 26, 1875-June 6, 1961) was a Swiss psychiatrist who founded analytical psychology.

Jean Jiraudoux (Oct. 29, 1882-Jan. 31, 1944) French novelist, essayist, diplomat and playwright.

Jean Johannes Jörjensen (Nov. 6, 1866-May 29, 1961): Danish writer, best known for his biographies of Catholic saints.

Jordan: the Hashemite Kingdom of Jordan is an Arab Kingdom in the Middle East.

James Joyce (Feb. 2, 1882-Jan. 13, 1941): Irish novelist and poet, considered to be one of the most influential writers in the early 20th century.

Johannesburg: also known as Jozi, is the largest city in South Africa, by population. It is the provincial capital of Gauteng, the wealthiest province in South Africa.

Jamaica: is an island country situated in the Caribbean Sea.

The Jogiellonian University: was established in 1364 by Casimir III the Great. It is the oldest university in Poland.

K

Kiel: is the capital and the most populous city in the northern state of Schlewig-Holstein.

Kvikne: is a former municipality in Hedmark and a mountain village between Østerdalen and Trøndelag.

Alexander Lange Kielland (Feb. 18, 1849-Apr. 6, 1906): is one of the most famous Norwegian realistic writers of the 19 century.

Klotzsche: is a district of Dresden, Germany.

Kalundborg: is a Danish city and the main town of the municipality.

Karylbo: is a part of the town Avesta in Avesta Municipality, Dalarna County.

Kechum: is a city in Blaine County, Idaho, U.S.A., in central part of the state.

Kilimanjaro: with its three volcanic cones, Kobo, Mawenzi, and Shira, is a dormant volcanic mountain in Kilimanjaro National Park, Kilimanjaro Region, Tanzania.

Krac ów: is the second largest and one of the oldest cities in Poland.

Kiev: is the capital and the largest city of Ukraine.

Nikita Khrushchev (Apr. 15, 1894-Sept. 11, 1971) led the Soviet Union during part of the Cold War. He served as First Secretary of Communist Party of the Soviet Union (1956-1964).

Kamakura: is a city in Kanagawa Prefecture, Japan

Hiroshi Kikuchi (Kan Kikuchi) (Dec. 26, 1888-March 6, 1848) Japanese playwright, novelist, and founder of the major publishing companies in Japan.

Kislovodsk: is a spa city in Stavropol Krai, Russia.

Knightsbridge: is a road which gives the name to an exclusive district in central London.

Orhan Kemal (Sept. 15, 1914-June 2, 1970) Turkish novelist.

Kermanshah: is in the western part of Iran and the capital of Kermanshah Province.

South Korea (The Republic of Korea): is a sovereign country in southern part of the Korean Peninsula.

Franz Kafka (Jul. 3, 1883-June 3, 1924) German-language writer of novels and short stories.

L

Jonas Lauritz Idemil Lie (Nov. 6, 1833-June 5, 1908): was a major 19th century Norwegian poet and playwright, and theatre director, who is considered to have been one of the Four Greats of 19th century Norwegian literature.

Giacomo Saverio Leopardi (June 29, 1798-June 14, 1837): Italian poet, essayist, philosopher and philologist.

Leipzig: is a city in the federal state of Saxony, Germany.

Liestal: is the capital of Liestal District and the canton of Basel-Country in Switzerland.

Lucerne: is a city in the north-central Switzerland, in the German-speaking portion of that county.

Lom: is a municipality in Oppland county, Norway.

Lillehammer: is a town and municipality in Oppland county, Norway.

Lübeck: The Hanseatic City of Lübeck is the second largest in Schlewig-Holestein, in northern Germany.

Legion d'honneur: is a French order established by Napoleon Bonaparte on May 19, 1802.

Lycée: a secondary school, especially in France, maintained by government.

Lebanon (Lebanese Republic) is a country in the East Mediterranean.

Latin America: the part of the American continents south of the United States in which Spanish, Portuguese, or French is officially spoken.

Arthur Lankvist (March 3, 1906-Dec. 11, 1991) Swedish writer, poet and literary critic.

Leoncia: is a village in east central Poland.

Lachine: is a former city on the Island of Montreal in south western Quebec, Canada.

Lithuania (the Republic of Lithuania) is a country in Northern Europe.

D.H. (David Herbert) Lawrence (Sept. 11, 1885-Arch 2, 1930) English novelist, poet, playwright, literary critic and painter.

Ezra Weston Loomis Pound (Oct. 30, 1885-Nov. 1, 1972) American poet and critic of the early modernist movement.

The University of Leeds: is a British Redbrick university located in the city of Leeds, West Yorkshire, England.

The Lost Generation: was the generation that came of age during World

War I.

M

The Maremma: is an extensive area of Italy bordering the Ligurian and Tyrrhenian Seas.

Mumbai, formerly known as Bombay, is the capital city of Indian state of Maharashtra. It is the most populous city in India (approximately 20.5 million).

Millaine: is a commune in the Bouches-du-Rhône in southern French in the former province of Provence.

Middlesex: is a historic county country in southeast England.

Mårbacka: is a mansion in Sunne Municipality in Wårmland, Sweden.

Munich: is the capital and the largest city of the German state of Bavaria.

Methuselah: according to Hebrew Bible, Methuselah is purported to be the oldest person to live.

Octave Mirabeau (Feb. 16, 1848-Feb 16, 1917) French journalist, art critic, travel writer, pamphleteer, novelist, and playwright, who achieved celebrity in Europe and great success among the public.

Michelangelo di Lodovico Buonarroti Simoni (March 6, 1475-Feb. 18, 1564) Italian sculptor, painter, architect, poet, and engineer.

The Modern Breakthrough: is the common name of the strong movement of naturalism and debating literature of Scandinavia which replaced romanticism near the end of the 19th century.

Madrid: is the capital and the largest city of Spain.

Massachusetts (Officially the Commonwealth of Massachusetts) is a state in the New England region of the northeastern United States.

Monmouthshire: is a county in south east Wales.

Modica: is a city and commune in the Province of Ragusa, Sicily, southern Italy.

Eugino Montale (Oct. 12-1896-Sept. 12, 1981) was an Italian poet, prose writer and translator.

Milan: is the second-largest city in Italy and the capital of Lombardy.

Benito Amil Andrea Mussolini (Jul. 29, 1883-Apr. 28, 1945) Italian politician, journalist and leader of National Fascist Party.

Málaga: is a city and a community and the capital of the Province of Málaga, in the Autonomous Community of Andalusia, Spain.

Madagascar (The Republic of Madagascar): is an island country in the Indian Ocean.

Prix Médicis: is a French literary award given each year in Norway.

Robert Gabriel Maugabe (Feb 21, 1924…) is the President of Zimbawe (Dec. 31, 1987).

Mexico City: is the Federal District, capital of Mexico, and the seat of the Mexican federal government.

Mexico (Officially the United Mexico State) is a federal constitutional republic in North America.

Antonio Cipriano Machado (Jul. 26, 1875-Feb. 22, 1939) Spanish poet and one of the leading figures of the Spanish literary movement—known as Generation of '98.

Nelson Rohihlahla Mandella (Jul. 18, 1818-Dec. 5, 2013): is a South African anti apartheid revolutionary and politician who served as President of South Africa from 1994 to 1999.

Somerset Maugham (Jan. 25, 1874-Dec. 16, 1965) British playwright, novelist and short story writer.

Murzzuschlag: is a town in northeastern Styria, Austria.

Mülheim Dramatists Prize: founded in 1976, is one of the leading theatre awards in Germany.

Mauritius (the Republic of Mauritius): became French colony in 1715 and was renamed Isle de France. It is an island nation in the Indian Ocean.

Montagnola: is a small Swiss village in Collina d'Oro municipality. It is located in the Italian-speaking canton of Ticino.

N

Immanuel Nobel, the younger (1801-1872) was a Swedish engineer, architect, inventor and industrialist.

Neo-romanticism: is used to cover a variety of movements in philosophy, literature, music, painting, and architecture, as well as social movements.

La Neuveville: is a municipality in the Jura bernois and administrative in the canton of Bern in Switzerland.

Norholm (Norholmen): is a manor house and agricultural property in Grimstad, in Aust-Agder county, Norway.

Nuoro: is a city and commune in central-eastern Sardinia, Italy.

New College, Oxford: is one of the constituent colleges of the university of Oxford in the United Kingdom.

Neuilly-sur-Seine: is a commune in the western suburbs of Paris, France.

New Albany: is a city in Floyd County, Indiana, U.S.A.

Friedrich Wilhelm Nietzsche (Oct. 15, 1844-Aug. 25, 1900) German philosopher, poet, composer, and cultural critic.

La Nouvelle Revue Française (The New French Review) is a literary magazine founded in 1909 by a group of intellectuals, including André Gide, Jacques Copea, and Jean Schlumberger.

Neo-Kantian: the philosophy of modern thinkers who follow Immanuel Kant in his general theory of knowledge.

Naples: is the capital of Campania and the 3rd largest municipality in Italy.

The New York Herald Tribune: was a daily newspaper created in 1924.

Norbotten County: is the northernmost county of Sweden.

Nigeria (The Federal Republic of Nigeria) is a federal constitutional republic comprising 36 states and its Federal Capital Territory, Abuja.

Nice: located on the southeast coast of France is the 5th most populous city in France.

Nitchdorf: is a commune in Timiş County in the Banat region of Romania.

Notre Dame University: is an independent, national Catholic university located in Notre Dame, Indiana, U.S.A.

O

Olshammar: is a locality situated in Askersund Municipality, Örebro County, Sweden.

Ordrup Station: is a station on S-train station in Copenhagen, Denmark.

The Order of Merit: is a dynastic order recognizing distinguished service in the armed forces, science, art, literature, or for the promotion of culture.

Oxford: is a county in central southern England.

Oak Park: is a village adjacent to the western side of the city Chicago in Cook County, Illinois, U.S.A.

Ottoman Empire, also historically referred to as the Turkish Empire or Turkey, was a contiguous transcontinental empire founded by Turkish tribes under Osman Bey in north-western Anatolia in 1299.

The Obie Award (Off-Broadway Theatre Awards) are annual awards given by Village Voice newspaper to theatre artists and groups in New York City.

Ontario: is one of the ten provinces of Canada, located in east-central Canada.

P

Pointe-à-Pitre: is the largest city of Guadeloupe, France.

Paul Mall Gazette: was an evening newspaper founded in London in February 7, 1865 by George Murray Smith.

Princeton: is a town in central New Jersey, U.S.A., located about 50 miles southwest of New York City.

Pacific Palisades: is a neighborhood district in the Westside City of Los Angeles, California, U.S.A.

Konstantin Georgiyevich Paustovsky (May 19, 1892-July 14, 1968) was a Russian Soviet writer nominated for Nobel Prize for literature in 1965.

The Phi Beta Kappa Society: is an academic honor society in the U.S.A., has 280 chapters.

Valentin Marcel Proust (July 10, 1871-Nov. 18, 1922) French novelist, critic, and essayist.

Penrhyndeudraeth (Peninsula with Two Beaches) is a village and community in the Welsh county of Gwynedd.

Puerto Rico (The Commonwealth of Puerto Rico) is an unincorporated territory of the U.S., located in the northeastern Caribbean.

Provence: is the geographical region and historical province of southeastern France.

Pindar: (c. 522-443 B.C.) ancient Greek lyric poet.

Parral: is a city and commune in the Linares Province of central Chile 7th region of Maule.

Parma: is a city in the Italian region of Emilia-Romagna.

Perranarworthal: is a civil parish village in Cornwall, England.

Zbigniew Preisner (Born: May 20, 1955 in Bielsco-Biala, Poland) is a Polish film score composer.

Peru (The Republic of Peru) is a country in western South America.

Princeton University: is a private Ivy League research university located in Princeton, New Jersey, U.S.A.

Padrón: is a community in the province of A coruña, in Galicia, Spain.

Q

Queen's University: is a public research university in Belfast, Northern Ireland.

R

Reichstag building: is the historical edifice in Berlin, constructed to house the German Imperial Diet, of the German Empire.

Maximilien François Marie Isidore de-Robespiere (May 6,

1758-Jul. 28, 1794) French lawyer and politician, and one of the best known and most influential figures of French Revolution.

Roquebrune-Cap-Martin: is a commune in the Alpes-Martimes department in southeastern between Monaco and Menton.

Radomosko: is a town in central Poland.

Randolph-Macon Woman's College: is a private liberal arts and science college in Lynchburg, Virginia, U.S.A.

Royal Military College at Sandhurst in Surrey is where all the officers in the British Army are trained.

Rekjavik: is the capital and largest city in Iceland. It is the world's northernmost capital of sovereign state.

Robinson Crusoe: is a novel by Daniel Defoe, first published on April 25, 1719.

Odilon Redon (April 20, 1840-July 6, 1916) French symbolist painter, printmaker, draughtsman and pastellist.

Yokomitso Riichi (March 17, 1898-Dec. 30, 1947) was an experimental, modernist Japanese writer.

Ruse (Rousse): is the fifth largest city in Bulgaria, located in the northeastern part of the country, on the right bank of Danube.

Franca Rame (July 18, 1928-May 29, 2013) was an Italian theatre actress, playwright and political activist.

Rondenbosch: is one of the Southern Suburbs of Cape Town, South Africa.

Royal Academy of Dramatic Arts: is a drama school located in London. It is one of the oldest drama schools in the United Kingdom, having been founded in 1904.

Rhodesia: was an unrecognized state located in southern Africa during the Cold War. From 1965 to 1979, it comprised the region now known as Zimbabwe.

French Riviera: is the Mediterranean coastline of the southeast corner of France, also including the sovereign state of Monaco.

S

Sanremo (San Remo): is a city on the Mediterranean coast of Liguria in north-western Italy.

Saint Petersburg: is a city and federal subject of Russia in the Neva

River at the head of the Gulf of Finland on the Baltic Sea.

Stockholm: is the capital and the most populous city in Sweden.

Sanskrit: is an ancient language that is the classical language of India and of Hinduism.

Collége Stanilas: is the name of three schools: Collége Stanislas in Paris, France; Collége Stanislas, with two locations in Quebec, Canada.

Sandymount: is an affluent coastal suburb in Dublin 4 on the Southside of Dublin, Ireland.

County Sligo: is located in the Border Region in Ireland.

Jonathan Swift (Nov. 30, 1667-Oct. 19, 1745) An Anglo-Irish satirist, essayist, political pamphleteer, poet and cleric.

Sardinia: is the 2nd largest island in the Mediterranean Sea.

Herbert Spencer (Apr. 28, 1820-Dec 8, 1903) English philosopher, biologist, anthropologist, and sociologist.

Sauk Centre: is a city in Streams County, Minnesota, U.S.A.

Mark Schorer (May 17, 1908-Aug. 11, 1977) American writer, critic, and scholar.

Charles Wharton Stork (Feb. 12, 1881-1971, born in Philadelphia) was an American author, a graduate of Haverford and Harvard, and taught in the Department of English at the University of Pennsylvania.

Sicily: is the largest on the southeastern coast of Sicily, Italy.

Scandinavia: is a historical and cultural-linguistic region in the Northern Europe and Sweden.

Oswald Arnold Gottfried Spengler (May 29, 1880-May 8, 1936) German historian and philosopher of history.

Louis: is an independent city and a major U.S. port on the eastern border of Missouri.

Sorbonne: is the seat of the faculties of arts and letters of the University of Paris.

Santruce: is one of the districts (barrios) of San Juan, Puerto Rico, and the biggest and most populated of all the districts in the capital.

William Shakespeare (April 26, 1564-Apr. 23, 1616) English playwright, widely regarded as the greatest writer in the English language.

Camilto Sharbaro (Jan. 12, 1888-Oct. 31, 1967) Italian poet.

Salinas Valley: is one of the major valleys and most productive regions in California, U.S.A.

Stalingrad: is the former name of Volgograd, a city in Russia.

Syria (The Syrian Arab Republic) is a country in Western Asia.

Sarajevo: is the capital of the largest city of Bosnia.

Joseph Stalin (Dec. 18, 1878-March 5, 1953) was the de facto leader of the Soviet Union from the mid-1920s until his death.

Santiago (Santiago de Chile) is the capital of Chile and the center of the largest conurbation.

Sydney: is the capital of New South Wales, Australia.

Gustav Sandgren (20 August, 1904-Aug. 11, 1985) Sweden author.

Särvast: is a village located in Boden Municipality, Norbotten County, Sweden.

Ernesto Camillo Sivori (Oct. 25, 1815-Feb. 18, 1894) Italian virtuoso violinist and composer.

Seville: is the capital and largest city of the autonomous community of Andalusia and the province of Seville, Spain.

Surfside: is a town in Miami-Dade County, Florida, U.S.A.

Sephardi: a Jew of Spanish or Portuguese ancestry.

Struga Poetry Evenings Golden Wreath: is an international poetry festival held annually in Struga, Republic of Macedonia.

Emiliano Zapata Salazar (Aug. 8, 1879-Apr. 10, 1919) was a leading figure in the Mexican Revolution, which broke out in 1910 against the president Porfirio Diaz.

Spring: is a city on the East Rand in the Gauteng province in South Africa.

Albert Sweitzer (Jan. 14, 1875-Sept. 14, 1965) was a German, and later--French theologian, musician, philosopher, physician and medical missionary in Africa.

Seoul: is the capital and largest metropolis of South Korea.

Seige of Leningrad (Leningrad Blockade) was a prolonged military operation undertaken by the German Army Group North against Leningrad.

Shandong: is a coastal province of People's Republic of China.

The National University of San Marcos: is the most important and espected higher-educational institution of Peru.

Ali Ahmad Said Esber (also known by the pen name Adonis or Adunis, born Jan. 1, 1930), is a Syrian poet, essayist, and translator. He has written more than 20 books and volumes of poetry in the Arabic language.

T

Tuscany: is a region in central Italy: formerly a grand duchy. The regional capital is Florence.

Thuringia (The Free State of Thuringia) is a federal state of Germany located in the central part of the country.

Count Lev Nikolayevich Tolstoy (Sept. 9, 1828-Nov. 28, 1910) Russian novelist, short story writer, playwright, and essayist.

Tours: is a city in central France, named after the Indre and the Lore rivers. It is also the site of the Paris-Tours road bicycle race.

Trelleck Grange: is a small hamlet in rural area of Monmouthshire, south east Wales, United Kingdom.

Trinity College: is a private, liberal arts college in Hartford, Connecticut, U.S.A.

Tbilisi (Tiflis) is the capital and the largest city in Georgia.

Aleksandr Trifonovich Tvardovsky (June 21, 1910-Dec. 18, 1971) Soviet poet and writer, chief editor of Novy Mir literary magazine from 1950 to 1954 and 1958 to 1970.

Tawfiq (Tawfik) al-Hakim (Oct. 9, 1898-July 26, 1987) was a prominent Egyptian writer. He is one of the pioneers of the Arabic novel and drama.

Trinidad: is an island in the Southeast West Indies. **Tokyo** (Tokyo Metropolis) is the capital and one of the 47 prefectures of Japan.

James Tait Black Memorial Prizes: are the literary prizes awarded for literature written in the English language.

Timiş: is a county of western Romania in the historical region of Banat.

Tunis: is the capital of both the Tunisian Republic and the Tunis Governorate. It is the Tunisia's largest city.

U

Uppsala University: is a research university in Uppsala, and is the oldest university in Sweden, founded in 1477.

Urla, Smyrna (Izmir) is a town and the center of the district of the same name in Izmir Province in Turkey.

UNESCO: United Nations Educational, Scientific and Cultural Organization: encourages international peace and universal respect by promoting collaboration among nations.

Uchiko: is a town located in Kita District, Ehime, Japan.

V

Vézelay: is a commune in the Yonne department in Burgundy in north central France.

Voronezh: is a city and administrative center of Voronezh Oblast, Russia, located on both sides of Voronezh River.

Vermont: is a state in the New England Region of the northeastern U.S.A.

Vicuña: is a Chilean commune in Elqui Province, Coquimbo Region.

The Vicuña (Vicugna) is one of the two wild South American camelids, along with the guanaco, which live in the high alpine areas of Andes.

Ambrose-Paul Valéry (Oct 30, 1871-July 20, 1945) is a French poet, essayist, and philosopher.

Växjö: is a city and the seat of Växjö municipality, Kronoberg County, Sweden.

Vietnam (Socialist Republic of Vietnam) is the easternmost country on the Indochina Peninsula in Southeast Asia.

Villeblevin: is a commune in the Yonne department in Burgundy in north central France. The town achieved prominence in 1960 when it was the site of the car crash that killed Albert Camus.

Paul-Marie Verlaine (March 30, 1844-Jan. 8, 1896) French poet associated with Symbolist movement.

W

Hugo Wolf (March 13, 1860-Feb. 22, 1903) Austrian composer of

Solvene origin, particularly noted for his art songs, or lieder.

Wola Okrzejska: a village in the administrative district of Genina Krzywda.

Warsaw: known in Polish as Warszawa is the capital and largest city of Poland.

Tennessee Thomas Lanier Williams III: (March 26, 1911-february 25, 1983) B. Columbus, MS   D. New York City, New York   Was an outstanding American writer who worked principally as a playwright in the American theatre.

West Virginia: is a U.S. state located in the Appalachian region of the Southern U.S.A.

Württemberg: The Kingdom of Württemberg was a state in Germany that existed from 1806 to 1818, located in the area that is now Baden-Württemberg.

Wehrmacht: was the unified armed forces of Germany from 1835 to 1945.

Colegio Williams (Williams College) is a private school in south-central Mexico City.

Wingham: is a community located in the municipality Huron Ontario, Canada.

Witwatersrand University: is a multi-camps in Johannesburg, South Africa.

West Indies: the British West Indies were united by the U.K. into a West Indies Federation between 1958 and 1962.

Y

Yelets: is a city in Lipetsk Oblast, Russia.

Yiddish: is a High German language of Ashkenazi Jewish origin spoken in many parts of the world.

Z

Zurich: is the largest city and the capital of Zurich, located in north-central Switzerland.

Mao Zedong (Dec. 26, 1893-Sept. 9, 1976) was the chairman of the People's Republic of China (1949-1991) and of the Chinese Communist party (1946-1973).

Sam Majdi

Author's Biography

Sam Majdi is a retired English teacher who has been living with his wife and children in Wichita, Kansas, U.S.A., for a long time. He has over 30 years experience in teaching English in high schools and colleges, more than 20 years managing and teaching in evening schools, and 30 years teaching English and some other subjects as a tutor. He studied two years in one of the few best teacher training colleges and got his teaching certificate and began his career as the assistant principal of high school for six years at the age of 18. After that he began studying in college, while teaching, in schools and evening schools and got his B.A. in English literature. He also studied two years for Master's degree in sociology and anthropology. Then he began teaching English in high schools and colleges for 20 years. He got over a dozen letters of recognition and a medallion from the government for his sincere services during all those years. He was always an advocate of human rights and freedom. He treated all his students with respect and kindness, no matter what grade and age they were. He has been a member of Kansas Authors Club in Wichita, Kansas, District 5 since 2001.

He self published his fist book ***Lovers Paradise Book of 222 Love Quotations*** in Newton, Ks, U.S.A., in 1997. After a very long time study and research his second book ***The Wisdom of the Great*** , a collection of 2650 quotations and biography, was published on demand by iUniverse in 2012. .

The third book, also a literary work, ***The Nobel Laureates in Literature,*** is the first and only collection about the lives, works, and achievements of 111 notables of the world who have been awarded Nobel Prizes in Literature since the beginning of 20th century (1901-2014). I hope you will like and enjoy reading these books. Please feel free to let the author know if you have any question, comment, or creative criticism. Your reviews mean a lot to the author. Sam Majdi

Email address: s_majdi@yahoo.com

40520135R00090

Made in the USA
Charleston, SC
05 April 2015